The Hunt for Ned October Illustrated

by

Bobby Legend

The Hunt for Ned October (Illustrated)
Published through Legend Publishing Co.

This is a work of fiction. Names, characters, places, and incidents are the product of the author's imagination or are used fictitiously. Any resemblance to actual persons, living or dead, events, or locales is entirely coincidental.

All rights reserved
Copyright © 2006 by Bobby Legend
Illustrations by Virginia Shuman

ISBN 978-0982-16875-2
No part of this publication may be reproduced, stored in a retrieval system, or transmitted in any form or by any means electronic, mechanical, photocopying, recording, or otherwise, without the written permission of the author or publisher.

INTRODUCTION

This is a suspenseful story about a six-year-old boy named Billy Smith, his mother, Marnie, a little, green turtle named Ned, Mr. Boyagian, the owner of Boyagian's Pet and Toy Store where Ned was purchased and two, devious Russian spies.

Billy left his friends one day
And moved to a home far, far away

Now Billy lives in a small, three-room home
And sits in his bedroom all alone

Now Billy's depressed and very sad
His mother wanted to make him glad

They both went shopping to change his day
"I wanted to make him happy," his mother would say

But before Billy and his mother entered Boyagian's store
A crowd of police exited through the front door

The police had arrested two Russian spies
To find out the truth from all of their lies

But Billy and his mother were unaware of the spies
And what they had done and entered Boyagian's store
To shop and have fun

You can buy a costume for Halloween
Whatever you want, I won't intervene

But Billy didn't want a costume that day
He wanted something different, he would say

So he decided to get something wet
And bought a little, green turtle for a pet

Now Billy was happy, with a smile on his face
As he carried his pet turtle in a small cardboard case

When he got home, he went right to his room
Then cleared a spot with a small broom

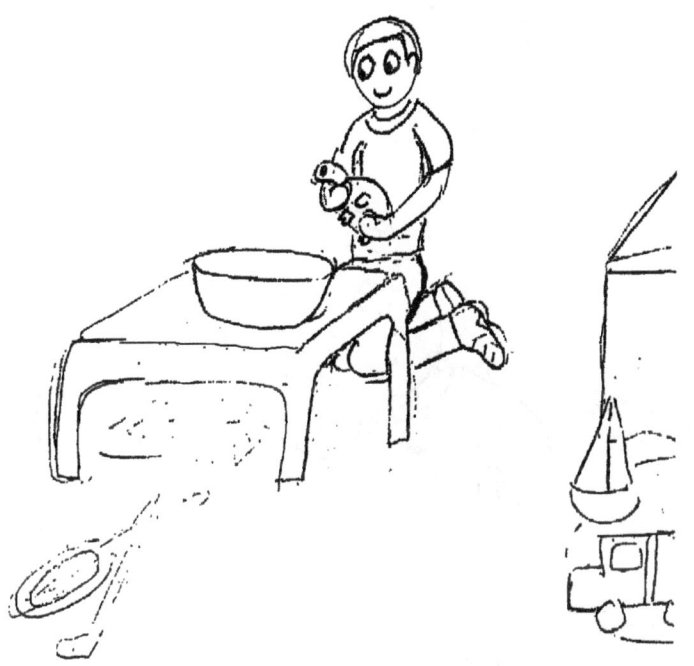

He placed his pet into its bowl near his bed
Then decided to call his pet turtle, Ned

Billy was so happy about his new friend
Oh, how he loved his pet turtle, Ned

But during a tussle with a neighborhood friend
They knocked over a table near Billy's bed

Ned was on that table, in his little bowl
And when he hit the floor, it took its toll

Ned hit the floor on the back of his shell
And blacked out when he fell

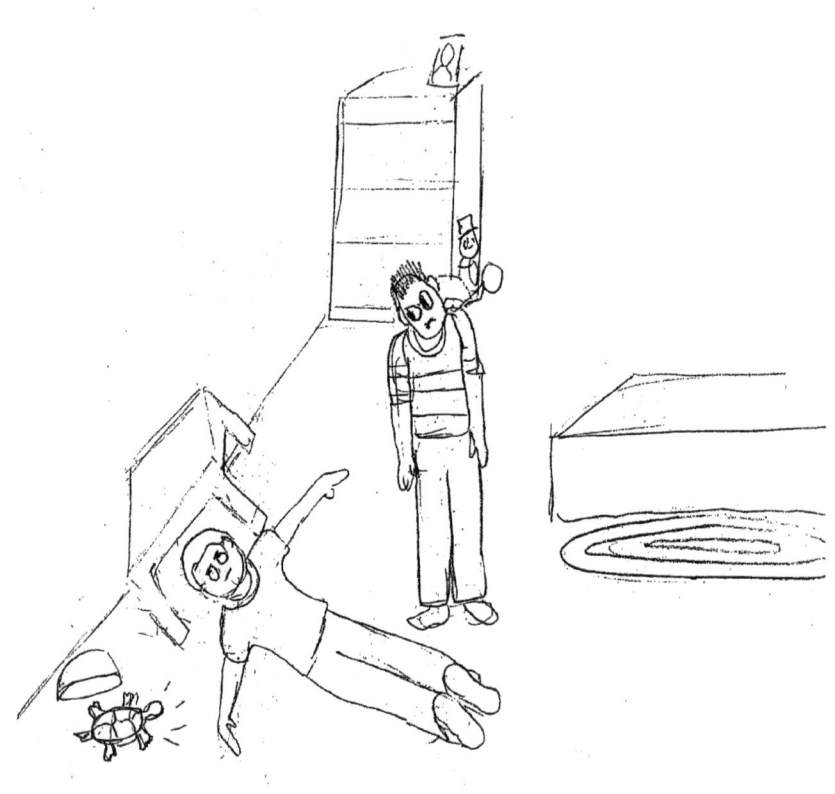

Due to the fight with his neighborhood friend
Both Billy and Ned were hit in the head

When Ned retreated into his shell
Billy was worried and gave a loud yell

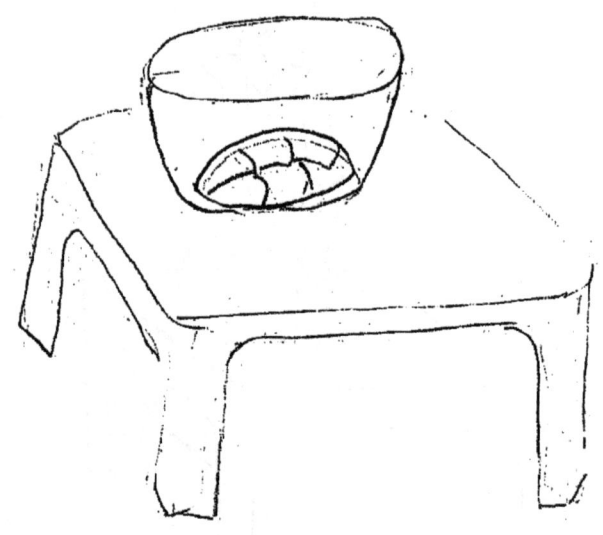

For Ned to come out to talk and play
But Ned was too sick for many a day

Both Billy and Ned became deathly ill
Nothing would help not even a pill

When Billy's illness gets much worse
He's rushed to the hospital before his head bursts

While Billy lay sick and on his death bed
He called for his buddy, his pet turtle, Ned

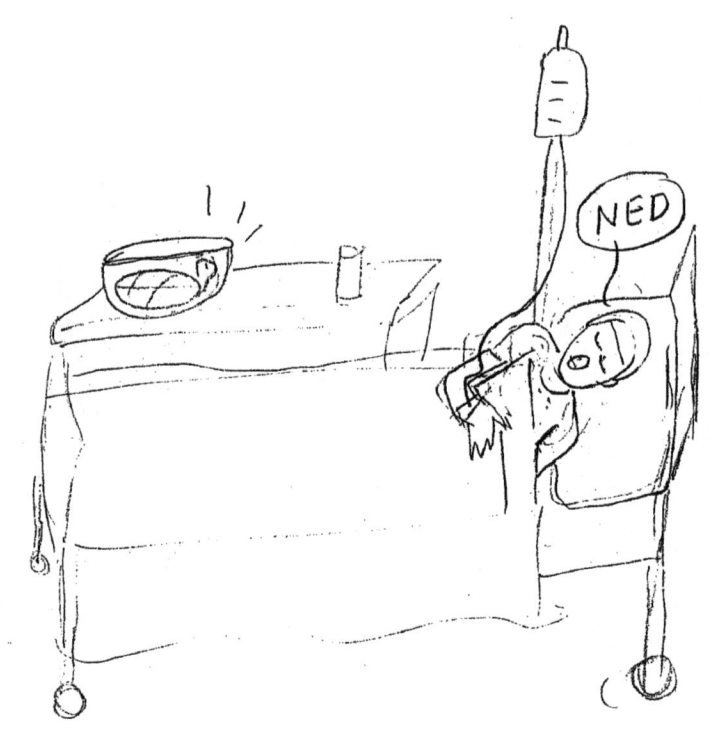

Ned must have heard Billy's yell
Because he awoke and came out of his shell

But suddenly Billy turned for the worse
When his injured head nearly burst

Now Billy lay comatose, almost dead
His mother tried one more thing, his pet turtle, Ned

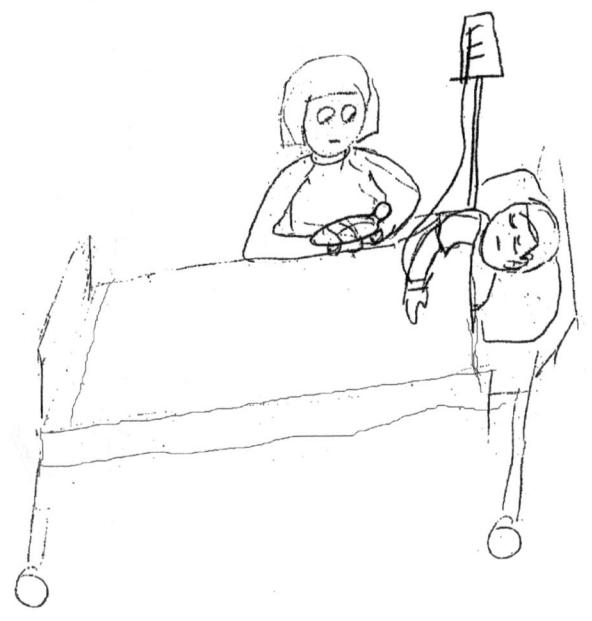

She placed little Ned on Billy's chest
Hoping to wake him out of his peaceful rest

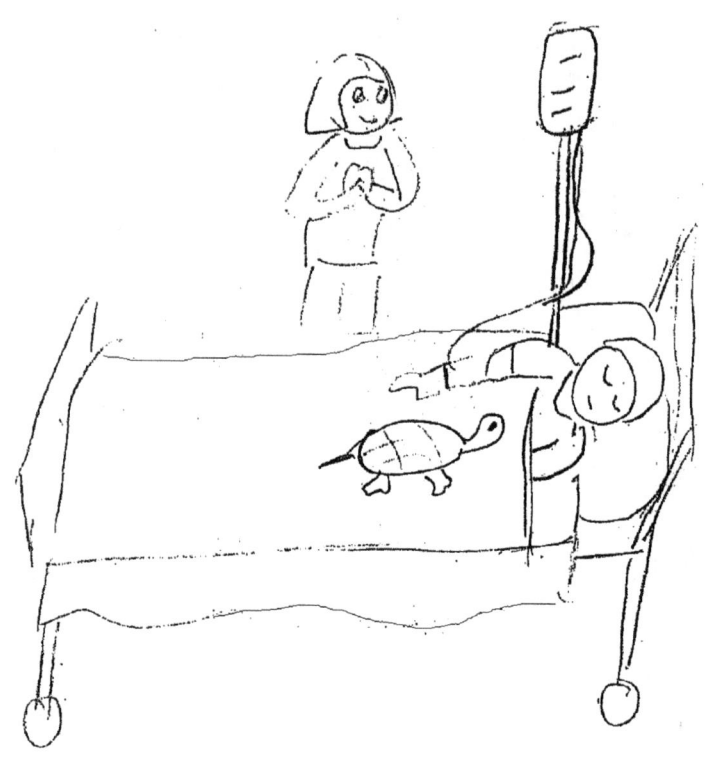

When Ned began to crawl on Billy
His mother wondered if it was silly

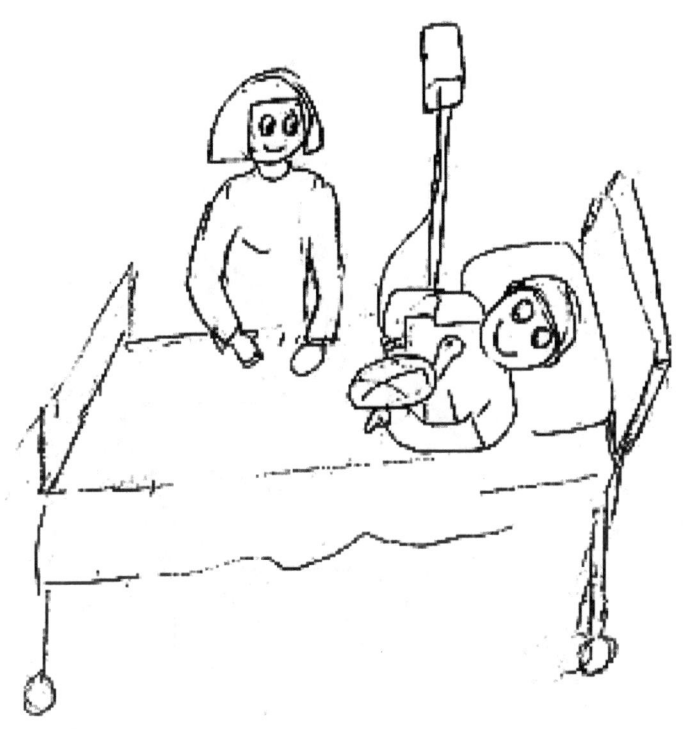

Billy must have felt his pet turtle, Ned
Cause he quickly awoke from the dead

Now Billy's at home thanks to Ned
Now the two are best of friends

But then one day, while cleaning out Ned's bowl
The poor little turtle went down a watery hole

Ned was flushed into a dark, watery grave
But somehow lived and was very brave

Ned fought for his life in the sewers below
Nearly fought to his death with a deadly foe

Ned escaped with his life and was out of breath
But continued on his journey with no fear of death

Billy was busy putting up flyers in town
And hoped his pet turtle would be found

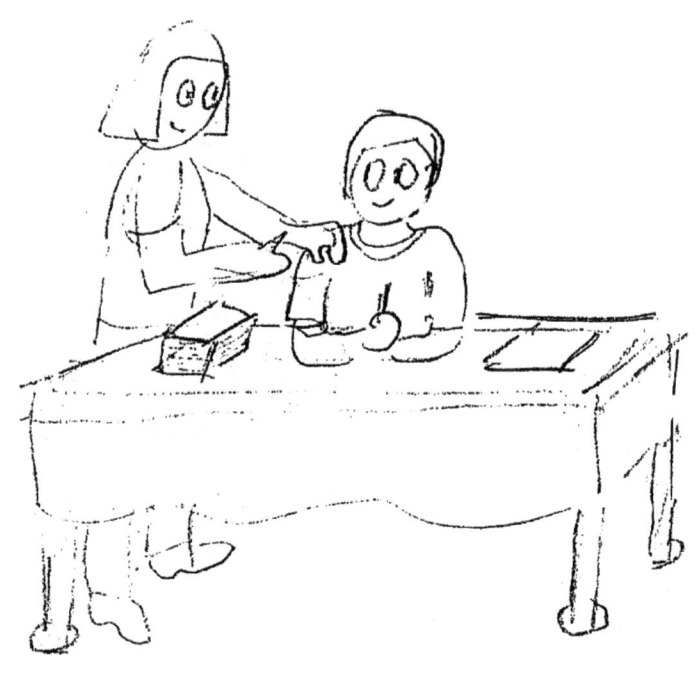

Never give up hope, Billy's mother would shout
Then Billy would smile instead of pout

Billy hoped and prayed everyday
Hoping his pet turtle would find his way

Billy wanted his pet back in his warm little bed
Oh how he loved his pet turtle, Ned

But two Russian spies got involved in the game

Wanting to find fortune and fame

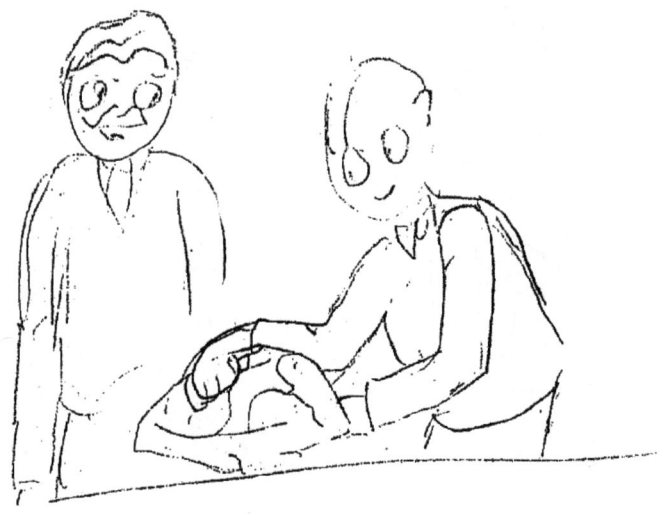

The two Russian spies got into the mix
When they injected a turtle with a precious micro chip

But the cops intervened and the spies were arrested
To have their stories and intelligence tested

But the cops had to let the Russians go
Lack of evidence, don't you know

When the spies were released and got off scot free
They had to find that chip before they could flee

So the spies went looking for their precious chip
That they had injected into one of those turtle's hips

But a hundred of Boyagian's turtles the spies would check
With a miniature fluoroscope, which was a pain in the neck

They had no luck finding the micro chip
That they had injected into a turtle's hip

But the spies continued on their quest
Searching and looking, they refused to rest

While the two spies searched high and low
Billy and Ned were always on the go

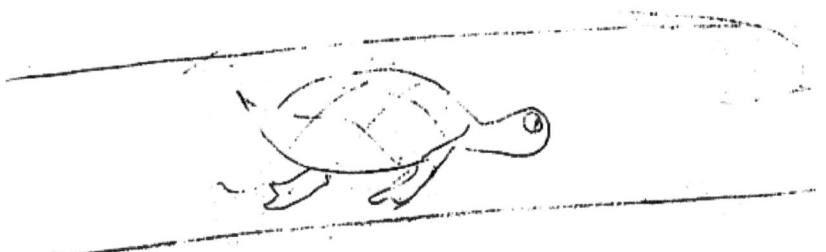

But weeks would pass and hopes would dim
For Ned to find his way home was very slim

But Billy listened to what his mother said
And continued to pray for the safe return of Ned

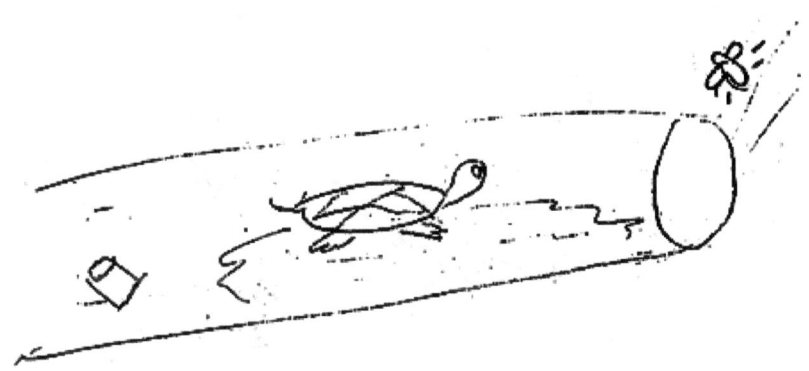

Finally, Ned had made progress and saw some daylight
Then fell into a pool that zapped his strength and might

But Ned was saved by a hippie bee
Brought him to land to set him free

Ned appreciated the help that he got
And Bobby Bee liked Ned a lot

That Bobby took Ned to his little campsite

To meet seven good-hearted insects that weren't too bright

But they soon became friends forever
And helped Ned in his endeavor

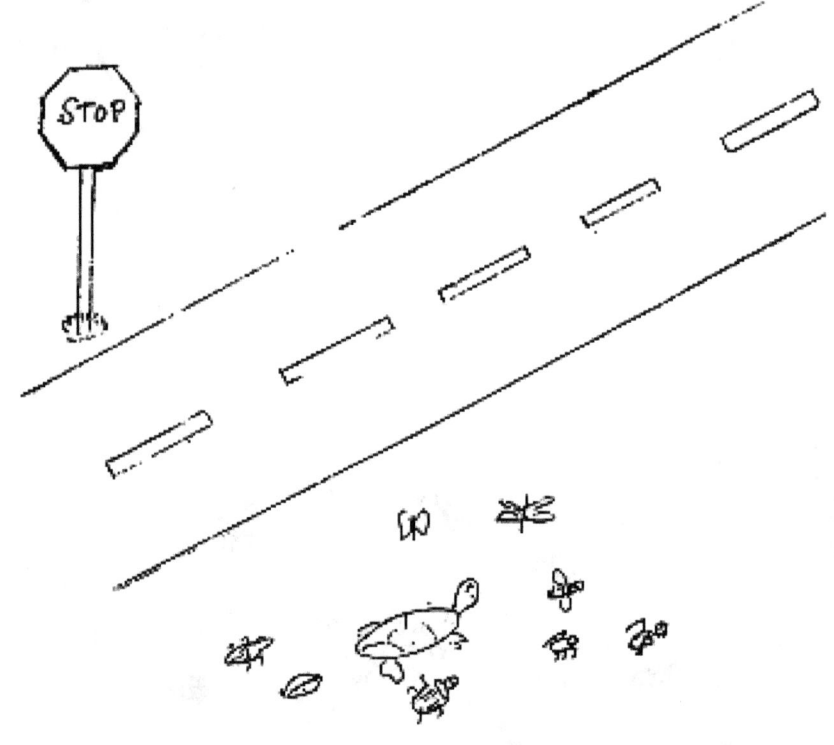

Ned crawled over land and many a road
Trying to find his owner's abode

But Ned would never give up
Or Billy might get himself a pup

But as time was short and winter grew near
Freezing to death was Ned's only fear

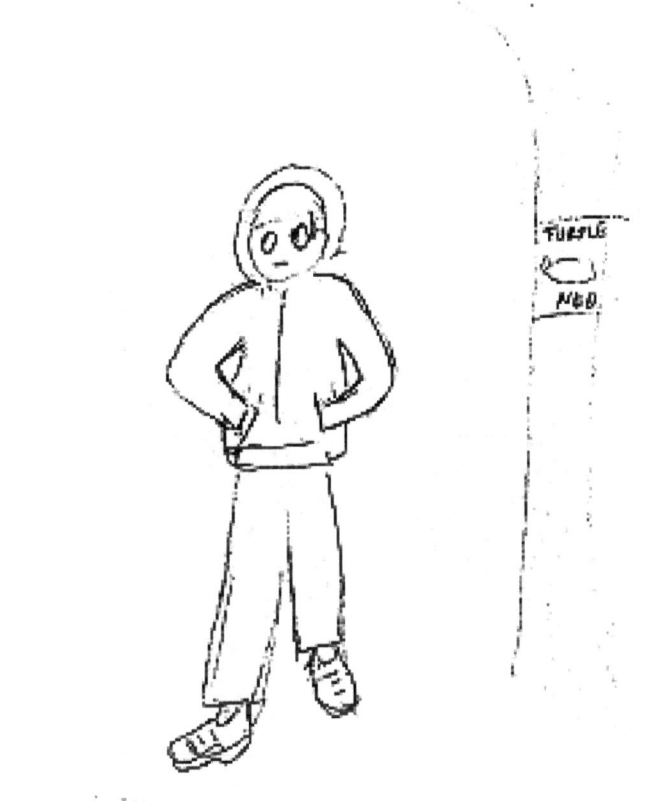

Then one day, Billy came by
But too far away for Ned to say, hi

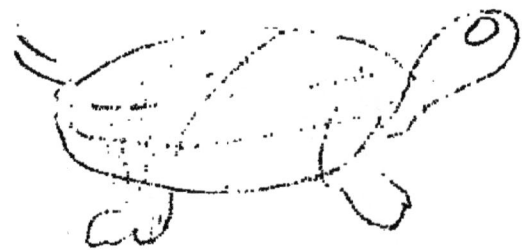

So Ned continued on his quest
Promising, never to rest

Eight little insects ready to fight
To help their friend Ned, with all their might

To get through the obstacles that lay in his way
And get Ned home, in just one short day

But trouble's lurking all around
Even while Billy's putting up flyers in town

The two Russian spies were looking for Ned
They didn't care if he was alive or dead

They did their best to find their chip

That they had injected into a turtle's hip

They looked and looked and had no luck
Then hit poor Billy with their truck

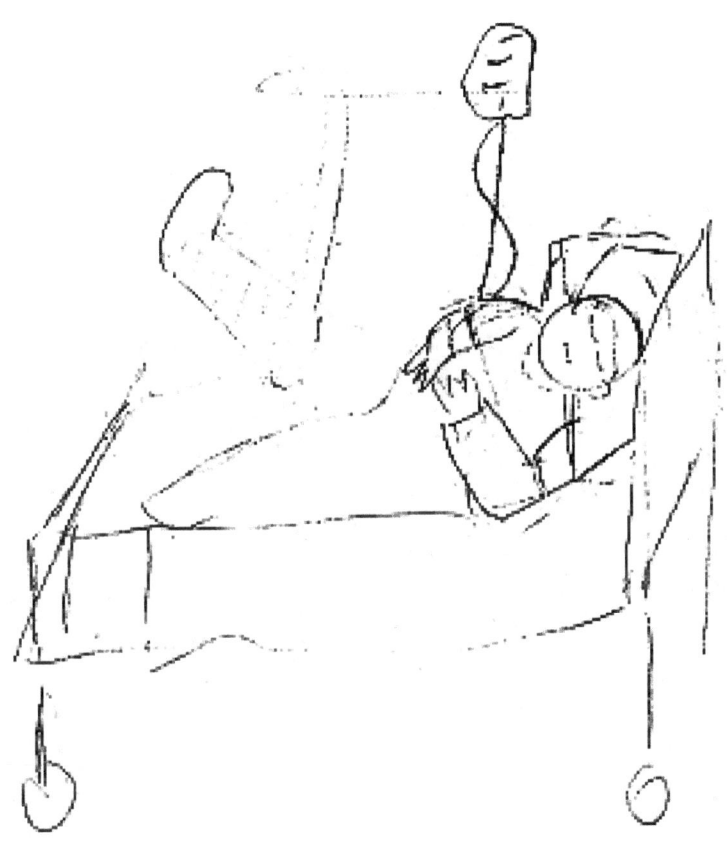

Billy was in traction in a hospital bed
When one of his friends found poor little Ned

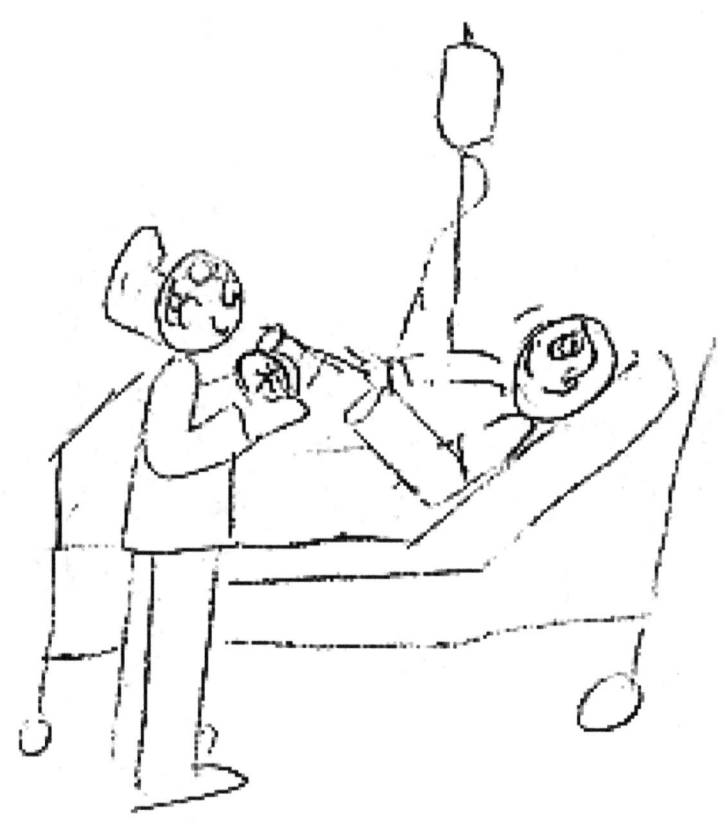

And brought the turtle to Billy's hospital bed
Then Billy saw his pet turtle, Ned

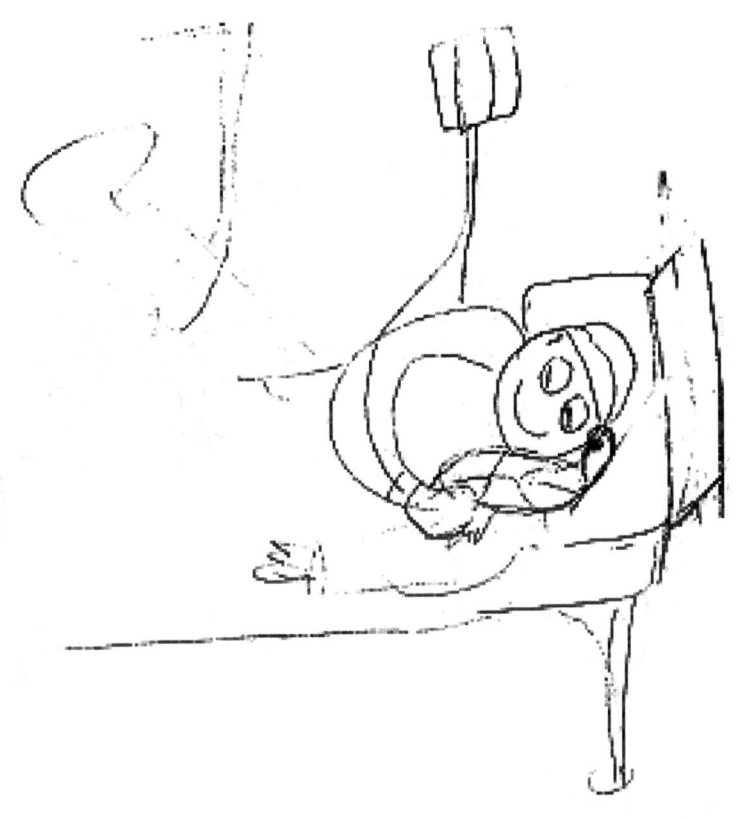

Ned cried for Billy and Billy for Ned

Billy always believed Ned wasn't dead

Billy and his turtle were in the hospital bed
When the two spies burst in to steal Ned

But the cops intervened and stopped their flight
Then deported the two without a fight

Now the two spies are in a Russian jail
Hoping one day that they will get bail

After a while, Billy carried Ned home

Then sat down and wrote this poem

Now Billy and Ned were happy again
But best of all, they're the best of friends

The moral to this story is never give up hope

Keep going forward don't just sit and mope

Keep plugging away at whatever you do
And good things will happen to you

CHAPTER 1

Six-year-old Billy Smith lives with his beautiful mother, Marnie and his only friend, a baby pet turtle named Ned October. Little Billy's father passed away suddenly from a heart attack not long ago and paying for his funeral and medical bills took most of their savings and left them strapped for cash. Billy's mother couldn't keep up with the mortgage payments on their beautiful house so they had to move into a much smaller home in a much poorer neighborhood. For this reason, Billy had to leave his school, neighborhood, and friends and move to the other side of town that was very far away.

Billy was sad and depressed when this happened, so his mother decided to take him shopping for a costume. It was October and close to Halloween. But Billy wasn't interested in trick-or-treating. He wanted to be with his old schoolmates and best friends again. He missed his old pal Ned who still lived in the old neighborhood. But poor Billy had moved too far away to be able to see him very often now.

On a warm, fall day, Billy and his mother walked to the local mall to shop for Billy's Halloween costume. As they approached the mall, they noticed a rather large crowd of people exiting through the doors of Boyagian's Pet and Toy Shop. But they were too far away to tell what was happening. By the time they had reached the mall, the excitement had died down and all was just about forgotten.

Billy was too immersed in his own little fantasy world wondering what he was going to buy to even care about anything else. But Billy's mom wondered what was going on so she decided to ask Mr. Boyagian, who was a friend and next door neighbor, about the crowd of people.

"What was all the excitement about, Mr. Boyagian?" asked Marnie.

"Oh, I don't really know. I think the police caught a couple of shoplifters and carted them off to jail," he said.

Billy's mother thought nothing more about the incident and went to the toy department across from the pet shop. While Marnie was looking over the costumes, Billy was busy looking at the pets in the pet shop. When his mother finally found her son, Billy no longer wanted a Halloween costume. He begged his mother for a baby turtle instead.

She reluctantly agreed to purchase the baby turtle for her son along with a bowl and the other supplies that were needed to raise it; but only on one condition.

"Billy, if you promise to clean the turtle bowl at least once every two weeks then you can have the turtle. Is it a deal?" asked Billy's mother.

"Yes Mom. I promise to keep the bowl clean," he said.

Billy was ecstatic with his new-found friend. He had a smile on his face for the first time in months, since his father passed away.

Billy and his mother left the shop with an armload of pet supplies and headed for home. Billy carried the little, green turtle in a small, white, cardboard box that the clerk had given to him at the pet shop. Billy constantly talked to his new friend on the way home, while his mother carried the rest of the supplies. She was happy to see her son with a big smile on his face.

Over the next few days Marnie would see a new attitude emerge in her son. He would once again become the happy-go-lucky boy that she had known before the death of his father and the move to their new home. And Marnie was very happy for her son.

When Billy got home, he went directly to his room and placed his pet turtle into the plastic bowl. He added water, gravel, and food, and then placed the bowl on the table near his bed. While lying on his bed, he watched and talked to his new friend. Suddenly, he came up with a name for his turtle. He decided to call him Ned October. He named him Ned after his old schoolmate and best friend, Ned and gave him the last name of October after the month he got the turtle. Billy was so happy with the name "Ned October" that he ran to the kitchen to tell his mother.

"Mom. Do you know what I named my turtle?" he asked.

"I don't know, honey. What do you call your new, little pet?" she asked.

"I call him Ned October. Do you know why?"

"Why?" asked his mother.

"Ned is for my friend from my school and October is for the month that I got him," said Billy.

"That's nice honey. Now why don't you go and play with your new friend," said Marnie.

Billy skipped back to his room and lay back down on his bed to watch and talk to his newfound friend, Ned October. He told Ned about anything and everything. Billy showed his little, green pal all of his favorite toys and even set up his soldiers around Ned's turtle bowl so they could guard him while he was sleeping. Billy loved his new pet.

While Billy talked, he watched Ned try out his new digs. Ned really loved the shade from the plastic palm tree that was placed on a tiny island in the middle of the bowl. He also liked the polished gravel because he didn't cut his little feet when he walked out of the water onto his island of paradise. Billy soon became infatuated with his friend.

Marnie began to worry about Billy. He begged his mom not to make him leave his room unless his turtle traveled with him. Because his personality had changed from one of being depressed and sad to one of joy and happiness, Marnie gave in to his pleas and let him have his own way. She let him stay in his room for long hours at a time to be with his turtle. She loved her son deeply and would rather see her son's smile than his tears. She knew it wasn't the right thing to do, but for the time being, she didn't think it would hurt him.

However, when it was time to return to school, Billy still refused to leave his turtle and threw a fit every time his mother tried to force him to go. He would only leave the house if Ned traveled with him. But the school refused to allow the turtle into his classroom except for special occasions like show-and-tell. Other than that, the turtle had to stay out of the classroom.

Well, Billy would have none of that. So his mother hired an in-house tutor, five days a week, paid for by the state, to teach Billy at home. Even while Billy was being tutored, he had to have the turtle on the table in front of him or he refused to study. But Billy's mother wasn't worried. After all, because of the turtle he was once again the happy son that he used to be.

CHAPTER 2

While little Billy Smith was getting acquainted with his new, little, green turtle the two people that had been arrested at Mr. Boyagian's Pet Shop were getting acquainted with the American criminal justice system. Mr. Boyagian thought they were just shoplifters but the police believed them to be spies and tried to question them about their activities.

"What were you two up to at Boyagian's Pet Shop?" asked Captain McCloud, as the two suspects sat quietly and unresponsive for a good minute until one of them spoke up.

"Why have we been arrested? We have done nothing wrong," snapped the male suspect.

"What are your names?" asked Captain McCloud.

"My name is Boris and hers is Nadia," he said. "We are Russian citizens and tourists in your country. Why are we being treated like this?"

"Treated like what? We just want to ask you a few questions," said Captain McCloud, as he stared intently into the male suspect's eyes.

"So ask your questions and then release us," snapped the female suspect.

"So, Nadia. You can talk. Let me ask you. What were you doing at Boyagian's Pet Shop?" asked Captain McCloud.

"We wanted to buy a puppy," she quipped.

"You really expect us to believe that? We believe that you two are Russian spies. Are you?" asked Captain McCloud.

"We are tourists. Nothing more," said Boris.

"We've been following you now for a number of days and we believe that you or Nadia has an important microchip hidden in your clothes or body. Would you allow us to search your persons?" asked Captain McCloud.

"If that will make you happy, by all means, search us," said Boris.

The two suspects were taken into a small room and searched one at a time: he by a male guard and she by a female guard. No incriminating evidence was found: only their passports to reveal their identities. They were returned to Captain McCloud for further questioning.

"I see by your passports that you're here on a tourist visa and your names are Boris Kolavski and your girlfriend's name is Nadia Romanelska. Is that right?" asked Captain McCloud.

"Yes that's right," said Boris.

"Now would you tell me the truth about why you were at Boyagian's Pet Shop?" asked Captain McCloud.

"We already stated why we were there. We wanted to buy a puppy," interjected Nadia.

"But we know that's not the truth, don't we?" asked Captain McCloud.

"Well, if you don't believe us we have nothing more to say," snapped Boris.

Captain McCloud continued asking questions but the two suspects refused to cooperate and remained silent. So they were placed in adjacent holding cells where they could speak to each other while the police ran a background check on them for any outstanding warrants.

"Now you two can think about your future, possibly behind bars," said Captain McCloud, as he locked the cell doors.

"We're innocent. Why are you doing this to us?" yelled Boris, as he grabbed the knob of the door and tried to shake it open.

"Quiet down. If you don't have any warrants you'll be out of here in a few hours," yelled Captain McCloud.

The two spies were moved to the detention room and pondered their future. They were worried that their boss might find out that they had been arrested and had lost their precious microchip. They talked about that very subject while waiting to be released.

"What are we going to do, Boris?" asked Nadia.

"We will sit here and relax until they release us."

"But once we're released we will have to tell our superiors

about our troubles and the loss of the microchip," said Nadia.

"No, we can't. I want fame and fortune, not the firing squad."

"But we must tell them about the chip," she said.

"Don't be absurd. Why do they have to know anything? All we have to do is find the chip and our troubles will be solved," said Boris.

"What do you suggest?" asked Nadia.

"When we leave here we'll return home, grab the miniature fluoroscope and then visit Boyagian's Pet Shop to check out the turtles. Using the miniature fluoroscope we will be able to detect which turtle has the chip. Once we find the right turtle, we'll buy it, take it home and take out the chip."

"That sounds good, Boris. But we were supposed to visit our embassy today and hand over the chip. We are already late and our superiors are probably wondering what has happened to us," said Nadia.

"But if we're released in the next few hours, we'll still have enough time to find the microchip," he said.

"I just hope your idea works."

"So do I, Nadia. So do I."

The police held them for nearly twenty-four hours before they had to release them due to a lack of evidence. Their passports were returned to them and they were allowed to leave. But Captain McCloud had the last word.

"We're gonna be watching you two. Sooner or later you're gonna mess up and then we'll have the evidence we need to lock you up forever," he said.

"I told you, Captain. We are only tourists. We have done nothing wrong," said Boris, as he smiled and walked out of the precinct, as Nadia followed.

Boris and Nadia went directly home to grab the miniature fluoroscope. Then they would return to Boyagian's Pet Shop to track down their precious microchip. But just as they entered their abode they were surprised to see their boss sitting in a chair and smoking a big cigar.

"Petrov, what are you doing here?" asked Boris.

"Please sit," he said, as Boris and Nadia sat on the couch in front of their boss.

"So why are you here?" asked Boris.

"I've been waiting for you. You and Nadia missed your appointment with me today at the Russian Embassy," said Petrov Kolakov, Russian Ambassador to the United States.

"Yes. We're sorry about that. But we ran into a little problem," said Boris.

"And what problem is that?" asked Petrov.

"We were picked up by the police and government agents and questioned," said Boris.

"And what did you tell them?" asked Petrov.

"Nothing. Absolutely nothing," said Boris.

"Good. Now what can you tell me about the classified work that you were hired to do for our Motherland? Do you have the microchip?" asked Petrov, smoking his cigar and filling the room with his smoke.

"I'm sorry to have to tell you this but we had to get rid of it just before our arrest," said Boris, nervously biting his fingernails.

"What? What are you saying? You blubbering idiots. We contract you to do a job and you lose the most important microchip in existence. How dare you. I should send you back to Russia and have you explain yourselves to my superiors. If I tell them that you lost the chip we will all be thrown into jail, or worse yet, we may be made into Russian stew," bellowed Petrov, puffing away on his cigar, until smoke covered his face.

"Please, Petrov. We didn't lose the chip, we just hid it," whined Boris.

"And where, may I ask, did you hide it?" asked Petrov.

"We injected the chip into a little, green turtle at a pet shop just a few minutes before the police arrested us," said Boris.

"You've got to be kidding. You two are unbelievable," said Petrov, shaking his head in disgust.

"Please, Petrov. Give us a chance to correct our mistake. All we have to do is return to the pet shop, find the right turtle and then take out the chip," said Boris.

"And how will you know which turtle has the microchip? Did you mark it? Or was there only one turtle in the store?" asked Petrov.

"No, there were many turtles in the aquarium. But we have a miniature fluoroscope that we can use to detect the chip. Then we'll buy the turtle, bring it here and take out the chip. That's all there is to it. We'll start right away if you give us the authorization. We should have the chip in your possession within seventy-two hours, unless the police or government agents follow us. Then it will take longer. But in the end we will accomplish our task," said Boris.

"Then I give you the go-ahead. But I don't care if it takes seventy-two days. I want that chip. Don't come back without it or you'll suffer the consequences. This is your last chance. Is that understood?" asked Petrov.

"Yes. We understand. We won't disappoint you," said Boris.

"You've already disappointed me. Just don't do it again," he snapped, then stood and walked to the front door.

"Thank you for understanding, Petrov. We won't let you down," said Boris, as he and Nadia watched their boss slam the door as he left their home.

"Nadia, we better find that microchip and find it fast. We only have a few days to accomplish our task," said Boris.

With that said, the two spies began making plans for locating and finding the turtle that held their precious cargo.

CHAPTER 3

As the weeks passed, Billy refused to meet the neighborhood boys. Instead, he chose to stay inside his bedroom and play and talk with Ned October. His mother and the tutor tried their best to talk to Billy about doing other interesting things besides staying in his room with his turtle, but he would have none of it.

"Billy, it isn't healthy to stay inside your room all the time. Why don't you go outside and play with the kids in the neighborhood?" asked his mother.

But Billy wouldn't listen. His life was centered on his buddy Ned October. Billy did keep his promise to his mother though. He cleaned Ned's turtle bowl every two weeks.

Billy would take Ned and the bowl into the bathroom, gently lifting Ned out of the bowl and placing him into the toilet as he set the dirty turtle bowl onto the sink for cleaning. Ned would swim around in the clean toilet water for a few minutes as Billy cleaned the bowl with a rag. Once the bowl was clean, Billy would then take Ned out of the toilet and place him back into the clean turtle bowl. Every time he cleaned the bowl, he replaced the old gravel with new gravel and fresh water. This chore took Billy only five minutes at the most, but he and turtle were quite happy afterwards.

As Billy continued to focus only on his turtle, Ned October, Marnie continued to worry about her son. So one day his mother asked a neighborhood boy who was the same age as Billy to come over to the house and meet her son.

"Billy. Come out of your bedroom. I have someone I want you to meet," she shouted.

Billy took his time before coming out into the hallway to meet this new boy. He didn't want to be away from Ned October any longer than he had to. From the way this boy was dancing around, as though he had ants in his pants, Billy wasn't at all interested in this boy his mom had brought home.

"Who are you?" asked Billy.

"I'm Tommy Lake. I live next door. Do you want to play?" he asked.

Billy just shrugged his shoulders as though he didn't want to be bothered.

"Billy, why don't you show Tommy your pet turtle?" asked his mother.

"Wow! Do you have a pet turtle, Billy?" asked Tommy.

"Yes."

"Can I see him?" asked Tommy.

"All right. I guess so. But you can't touch him," said Billy as they walked to Billy's bedroom.

While Billy and Tommy were getting acquainted, Marnie busied herself making something to eat for the boys. She made them soup and sandwiches.

As the boys entered Billy's room, Billy quickly set down the rules.

"Okay Tommy, if we're going to be friends, you better not get too close to my turtle. He's my friend and nobody else's. Understand?" asked Billy.

"Why are you being so touchy Billy? It's just a crummy, old turtle," said Tommy.

"You take that back. He's not a crummy, old turtle. He's my best friend and you can't talk about him that way," yelled Billy.

"I'm sorry. I didn't mean anything by it. What's your turtle's name?" asked Tommy.

"Ned. Ned October. I bought him at Mr. Boyagian's Pet and Toy Shop just a few weeks ago," said Billy.

"Why do you have all your toy soldiers around his bowl?" asked Tommy.

"They are protecting him from enemies. They guard him when I leave the room or when I'm sleeping," said Billy. The two boys stood over the bowl, watching Ned swim in his little pond.

"Is your turtle a boy or a girl?" asked Tommy.

"His name's Ned. That's a boy's name silly," said Billy as the two boys got better acquainted.

The two boys sat on Billy's bed and watched Ned while they talked about Christmas which was only a few months away.

"What are you getting for Christmas Billy? What do you want Santa to bring you?" asked Tommy.

"I haven't thought about it that much. I've been too busy playing with Ned. He's my best friend," said Billy.

"He's just a pet turtle. How can he be your friend when I'm your friend?" asked Tommy.

"Ned's my friend. I don't even know you. I just met you today," said Billy.

"Does Ned talk back to you like I do?" asked Tommy.

"Yes. I talk to him and he talks to me. We talk to each other all the time," said Billy.

"Let me hear him talk to you," said Tommy.

"He won't talk to me if someone is listening," said Billy.

"He can't talk. He's just a dumb turtle. You just pretend he can talk to you," said Tommy.

"You're wrong! He can talk to me," said Billy. Just then the two boys began to wrestle on the bed, angry over the conversation that had taken place.

As the wrestling became more and more aggressive, the boys rolled off the bed and onto the floor. Suddenly, one of them kicked the table next to Billy's bed and knocked Ned and his bowl onto the floor.

When Billy saw what had happened, he rolled off of Tommy and crawled over to check on the well-being of his pet turtle. While he was checking Ned's pulse, Tommy ran out of the bedroom, out of the house and straight to his own home. He wanted nothing more to do with Billy or his pet turtle.

When Marnie heard the loud noise, she ran into Billy's bedroom to see what all the commotion was about.

"What happened honey?" asked Marnie as she viewed the overturned end table and other wreckage that lay all over the bedroom floor.

"Boy, you two certainly made a mess in here," said Marnie, as she began picking up the mess.

"Mom, Ned is hurt. He won't move. Something is wrong with him," said Billy. He held out his outstretched palm showing her his pet turtle.

"He'll be all right, dear. He's just in shock from falling onto the floor. He fell more than three feet. That's like falling off a cliff to him," said Marnie.

"What can I do to make Ned better?" asked Billy.

"Put him back into his bowl after you replace the water and gravel. Then we'll see how he is in the morning. If he's not better, we'll take him back to the pet shop and see if the clerk or Mr. Boyagian can give him some turtle medicine to make him well. But I'm sure Ned will be better by morning," said Marnie. She then helped Billy with the gravel, leaving the room to retrieve a cup of water.

When she returned, she poured the water into the turtle bowl and watched her son gently place Ned onto his little island. But Ned didn't move. His hands, feet, and head were immersed in his shell. Marnie couldn't tell if Ned was dead or not. She hoped and prayed that he wasn't. She knew that if Ned died Billy would most likely revert back to the sad little boy he was before he got the turtle.

Billy and his mother kept an all-night vigil by Ned's turtle bowl, looking for any slight movement or possible change. Billy didn't sleep at all that night. He constantly prayed for his little friend's health to return. He asked his toy soldiers to fight off Ned's invisible injury and to take his pain away. The soldiers listened to Billy intently as they stood silently at attention, weapons drawn and ready to use at a moment's notice.

But morning came and Ned was lethargic as ever. Billy was very worried and upset. Ned wouldn't even stick his head out of his shell to say hello. Billy didn't know what to do. He ran out of the room, like Flash Gordon, and went to find his mother. She was in the kitchen making them breakfast.

"Slow down mister. What's wrong? How is Ned this morning?" asked Marnie.

"He's still sick. I don't know what's wrong with him. He won't come out of his shell. He didn't say hello to me this morning. I know something's wrong," cried Billy.

"Calm down Billy. I told you yesterday, if Ned wasn't any better come morning, we'd take him to the pet shop and have the clerk fix him up," said Marnie.

"I'll get my coat and we can leave as soon as I put Ned in his carrying case," said Billy as he turned to run to his bedroom.

"Wait a minute, Billy. You sit down here and eat your breakfast first. Then we'll take Ned to the pet shop."

"But mom, Ned might die if we don't get him to the doctor right now," cried Billy.

"Billy, I know you're scared, but if you don't eat, you'll get sick too. Ned can wait until you do that. Now eat," said Marnie as she placed a plate of scrambled eggs and bacon in front of him.

Billy ate as fast as he could without choking on his food, like a human vacuum cleaner because his little friend's life was at stake. He didn't want to waste any more time than he had to. Within two minutes, he had gobbled down his food in record time.

"I'm finished. Can we go now?" asked Billy.

"Drink your milk first. Then we'll go," said his mother.

Billy quickly drank his milk in one long gulp. When he was finished, he slammed the empty glass onto the table and ran to his room to get his turtle and winter coat.

"I'm ready," said Billy, holding the little, cardboard carrying case that contained Ned October.

"You know Billy, tonight's Halloween. Are you going to go trick-or-treating?" asked his mother.

"I don't think so. Ned is too sick to be taken outside to beg for candy. Anyway, I don't have a costume," said Billy as he waited for his mother to put on her winter coat.

"We can make you a costume. How about a bum or a clown or maybe a pirate? What do you want to go as?" asked Marnie.

"I don't care. I want Ned to get better. Then I'll worry about Halloween," said Billy. They walked out the front door and into the fall weather.

Billy and his mother walked the two blocks to the mall where Mr. Boyagian's Pet and Toy Shop was located. Billy kept his little pet turtle inside his coat right next to his heart. He was anxious to see Mr. Boyagian. After all, he knew how to fight for survival because he had been an Armenian holocaust victim at the hands of Turkish soldiers. Billy hoped he had a magic potion that would help his pet turtle fight as well.

The second Billy entered the pet shop he ran up to the counter where Mr. Boyagian was standing.

"Mr. Boyagian, I need your help," cried Billy.

"What can I help you with son?" asked the ninety-eight-year-old man.

"My turtle that I bought from you three weeks ago fell off my table and is sick. Can you give him some medicine for his illness?" asked Billy. He then reached into his coat and pulled out the tiny, cardboard box that contained his pet turtle, Ned October.

Billy took the top off the box and placed it on the counter. Mr. Boyagian peered down into it and saw a docile and still shell.

"All I see is a shell. Are you sure the turtle is in there?" asked Mr. Boyagian, peering over his thick glasses.

Billy reached up and tipped the box to make sure his turtle was still in its shell.

"Yeah, he's in there. He's just not feeling good enough to come out," said Billy. He looked into Mr. Boyagian's eyes, pleading for a cure.

"Well, let me take a look," said Mr. Boyagian as he picked up the sickly turtle.

Mr. Boyagian held the small turtle up to his eyes to see if it was still alive. When he touched the head with his finger, the turtle gave a little nudge. So Mr. Boyagian knew the turtle was still alive.

"Will he be all right? He won't die, will he?" asked Billy.

"Oh, I think he'll be all right. How did he get hurt?" asked Mr. Boyagian as he checked out the little turtle.

"He fell from a three-foot-high table and landed on his back," said Billy.

"He got shell shock, that's all. He's going to need a lot of rest and good care. I think I have some medicine that I can give him. That should help him until he gets on his feet," said Mr. Boyagian. He filled a small eyedropper with some vitamins and fed them into the sick turtle's mouth.

"Will that stuff make him better?" asked Billy.

"I think it will. But he needs rest. So when you get him home put him into his bowl and don't touch him until he starts walking again. That should take one or two weeks at least. So you'll have to be patient. Can you do that son?" asked Mr. Boyagian.

"I think so. I have to be if I want Ned to get better," said Billy.

Mr. Boyagian then returned Ned to his carrying case and closed the lid. He handed the box to Billy and did not charge them for his services.

"Is Ned your turtle's name?" asked Mr. Boyagian.

"Yes, I call him Ned October," said Billy.

"That's a nice name. Remember, have patience," said Mr. Boyagian.

"Thank you Mr. Boyagian," said Billy's mother.

"Yeah, thank you," added Billy.

"Let me know how he's doing. Will you do that Billy?" asked Mr. Boyagian.

"I sure will," said Billy as he and his mother walked out of the store.

CHAPTER 4

Billy and his mother remained hopeful as they walked back from the pet shop, wondering when Ned would feel better. As soon as they returned home, Billy took Ned out of his box and put him back in the turtle bowl. Ned still refused to come out of his shell.

Billy took off his coat and lay on the bed. He stared intently at Ned, watching and hoping that his pet's health would soon return. Billy stayed in his room all day and night. He even refused to get dressed up for Halloween. While his mother was busy handing out candy to the neighborhood children, Billy was in his bedroom praying for Ned October.

In the meantime, Marnie had again invited Tommy over to the house. Because he was the one who fought with Billy and caused the injury to Ned, she wasn't sure how he would react to seeing Tommy again. But she wanted the two boys to shake hands and try to become friends.

Marnie escorted Tommy into her son's bedroom so Tommy could show Billy his Halloween costume hoping that her son would want to go out trick-or-treating. But things got out of hand immediately upon Tommy's entrance into the room. The second Billy saw Tommy he jumped off his bed and ran directly at the boy that had caused his pet's injury.

Billy grabbed Tommy by the neck and the two boys began to fight as Marnie tried to intervene and break up the skirmish. But the boys refused to listen to Marnie's shouts and fell to the floor still clutched in a wrestling hold. They began rolling on the floor when suddenly the boys once again kicked the table where Ned's turtle bowl sat.

This same incident to Ned happened again. But luckily, just as the table fell to the floor, Billy's mother grabbed the turtle bowl before it went flying across the room. Marnie saved Ned from being severely injured again. Even though the little, green turtle had been shaken up and tossed around the room, he still seemed to be okay for the moment. But Billy was another matter.

Before the table fell to the floor, it came down hard on little Billy's head with the corner's edge clipping him behind his left ear. But the two boys continued fighting and wrestling.

After Billy's mother picked up the table and returned Ned and the turtle bowl to the right place, she grabbed the boys by their earlobes, squeezing them until they calmed down and returned to normal.

"Break it up. What's wrong with you two? Billy, you ought to be ashamed of yourself. What were you thinking when you attacked Tommy?" asked Marnie.

"I don't know. He hurt my Ned and I wanted to hurt him," said Billy giving Tommy a dirty look.

"I want you to apologize to Tommy right now for attacking him. He came here as your friend to show you his Halloween costume. He thought you might want to go out trick-or-treating with him. But now you'll have to stay in your room and think about what you have done. You're lucky Ned is still alive," snapped Marnie.

"I'm sorry, Tommy," said Billy, as the two boys shook hands.

"That's all right," said Tommy.

Tommy and Marnie left Billy's bedroom while Billy picked up the toy soldiers and placed them around Ned's turtle bowl to protect him from harm. Then he lay back on his bed and talked to his little friend while rubbing his bruised and hurting head.

"I'm sorry, Ned. I didn't mean to hurt you again. I promise not to disturb you again until you're well," said Billy.

Billy stayed up nearly the whole night until he finally fell asleep around daylight. Ned stayed in his shell and refused to come out to play with his little friend. Billy's mother didn't know what to do with her son. He refused to leave his room until his pet was well again. Even when his tutor came to give him lessons, he refused to be taught any place but in his room. So the tutor had to teach Billy in his room so he could be close to his turtle.

The day after Billy and Tommy's slugfest, Billy was feeling

very dizzy and his head still hurt. But he ignored the pain and put on his leather pilot's cap and winter coat and sneaked out of the house without his mother's knowledge. Billy wasn't satisfied with Mr. Boyagian's remedy for Ned so he took it upon himself to get some more help. He packed his pet turtle into the carrying case and walked back up to the pet shop.

Billy entered the pet shop and went directly to the old man behind the counter.

"Mr. Boyagian, your medicine didn't help my turtle at all. Would you please give him the correct stuff? Ned is still in shell shock," said Billy. He opened up the cardboard case and showed Mr. Boyagian that his turtle was still sick.

"So your turtle didn't take to my medicine, huh? Well, I'll try something else, but I can't promise anything. It's just going to take time for your pet to get better. He needs a lot of bed rest. You need bed rest when you're sick don't you?" asked Mr. Boyagian, picking up Ned and feeding him another liquid diet of turtle antibiotics.

"Will that stuff help Ned this time, Mr. Boyagian?" asked Billy.

"I hope so. Remember, your little friend here needs a lot of rest and relaxation," said Mr. Boyagian. He placed Ned back into his carrying case and closed the lid.

"Thank you Mr. Boyagian," said Billy. He grabbed Ned's carrying case and walked out the pet shop door heading for home.

Billy made it back home and into his bedroom without his mother knowing that he had left the house. The minute he entered his bedroom, he quickly shut the door and placed Ned back into his turtle bowl. Then he took off his cap and coat and threw them onto his bed covering his pillows.

Billy sat down on the edge of his bed and began talking to Ned. But after a few minutes, Billy was tired and laid down to rest. He noticed his white pillowcase had red spots on it when he moved his cap and coat off the bed. Realizing the stains were from his head wound, he quickly took the pillowcase off his pillow and hid it from his mother in his toy box. He didn't want her to know that he had been hurt during his fight with Tommy. Once Billy had hidden the evidence, he went back to bed and took a little nap.

Later that day, Marnie noticed her son wasn't acting normally. He was acting rather lethargic and was sleeping constantly.

Marnie figured it was just her son's reaction to Ned's injury. But then, while putting Billy's toys away, she found Billy's white pillowcase stained with blood hidden inside the closet. She confronted him about the bloody pillowcase and he tried to change the subject. But Marnie wanted to know the truth. She looked over her son's body and found a swollen wound behind his left ear.

"What happened, Billy? How did you injure your head?" asked his mother.

"It got cut when Ned's table fell on me the other day as Tommy and I were fighting," said Billy, rubbing his teary eyes.

"Why didn't you tell me your head was cut? We need to get your wound looked at and cleaned. I'm going to run next door to see if Mr. Boyagian is home. He used to be a doctor in his old country. Maybe he can help us. I don't have the money for a doctor," said Marnie as she felt his forehead to see if he had a fever.

"I'm okay mom," said Billy. And he walked over and sat on his bed.

"Your forehead is warm. I think you have a slight fever. I'm going to see Mr. Boyagian right now," said Marnie.

She walked over to Mr. Boyagian's house and knocked on his front door. Within a few minutes, the pet shop owner opened the door.

"Can I help you Marnie?" asked Mr. Boyagian.

"Mr. Boyagian, I know it's late, but could you come over and take a look at my son. He hurt himself the other day and he has a slight bump and small cut behind his left ear. I thought you being a doctor once, could help him," said Marnie.

"Can't you take him to your family doctor?" asked Mr. Boyagian.

"Not really. I can't afford it right now. If you think he should go to a doctor, I'll take him. But would you look at him first? Maybe you could treat his head wound?" asked Marnie biting her lip.

"Yes, I'll help if I can. What happened to him? What part of his head did he injure?" asked Mr. Boyagian as he and Marnie walked back to her house.

Marnie explained the situation to Mr. Boyagian as she escorted him into the house, directing him towards Billy's bedroom. When they entered, Billy was laying on his bed. His face was sunken and pale.

"Billy, Mr. Boyagian is here to take a look at your injury. He thinks he can make your boo-boo go away," said Marnie.

"Hello Billy. Your mother tells me you're not feeling well and you've injured your head. Let's just see if I can't make you feel better. Why don't you show me where you're hurt?" asked Mr. Boyagian as he sat on the bed next to Billy.

Little Billy slowly turned his head to show Mr. Boyagian his swollen and infected wound.

"Billy also has a slight fever," said Marnie.

Mr. Boyagian felt Billy's forehead. "Marnie, would you please boil me some water and bring me some Epsom salt, a large bandage, a gauze sponge, a piece of cotton, alcohol, and a thermometer. That is if you have them," said Mr. Boyagian.

"I think I have most of the stuff," said Marnie. She left the room to track down the items Mr. Boyagian had asked for.

Within a few minutes, Marnie had returned with the items needed to clean Billy's wound and handed them to Mr. Boyagian. First, Mr. Boyagian placed the thermometer into Billy's mouth and then swabbed his wound with a cotton ball doused in alcohol. Then he dipped the gauze sponge into the hot water, put a bit of Epsom salt onto it and placed it over the wound to draw out the infection. Then he held it on with a large bandage. Now they would have to wait and see.

Mr. Boyagian checked the thermometer.

"Marnie, Billy does have a slight fever, so keep an eye on him. I'll check back in two days. If he doesn't get any better, then you might want to take him to your family physician. But if you need me for anything don't hesitate to call on me. I'm always happy to help. And you, young fella, must get some rest and stay in bed until you get well," said Mr. Boyagian. He patted little Billy on the leg then covered him up with the blanket.

"Thank you, Mr. Boyagian. I don't know how I can thank you," said Marnie.

"I'm glad I could be of some help. By the way, how is Billy's pet turtle doing?" asked Mr. Boyagian, as Marnie escorted him to the front door.

"Ned's not doing so good either," said Marnie.

"I'm sorry to hear that," he said.

After Mr. Boyagian left, Marnie returned to her son's bedroom to see how he was doing. She peeked into his room and saw her son sound asleep. So she turned off the light and closed the door.

Marnie prayed that her son and his pet turtle, Ned October, would get well very soon. She was sure that she would see Billy in better spirits if he knew that Ned was over his illness.

But over the next two days, Billy's illness turned much worse. His fever became dangerously high and he was in and out of consciousness for hours at a time. Marnie was very worried that her son might die if something wasn't done immediately.

Marnie again turned to Mr. Boyagian for help. He saw the shape Billy was in and decided he needed to be in the hospital. His mother picked up Billy from the bed and carried him to his car, with Mr. Boyagian following close behind. They drove straight to the emergency room of the local hospital two miles away. When the receptionist saw how sick Billy looked, he was taken directly into the emergency room and placed on a gurney.

The emergency room doctor began treating Billy's swollen and infected head wound immediately. He gave Billy mega doses of antibiotics to bring down the fever and swelling. While Billy was being treated, his mother and Mr. Boyagian were sitting outside in the waiting room hoping and praying for Billy's health to return.

Marnie was going crazy not knowing how her son was doing. She was a nervous wreck by the time the doctor came out to speak with her thirty minutes after Billy had arrived at the hospital.

"Miss, I'm Dr. Stevens. Are you Billy's mother?" asked the doctor.

"Yes, I'm Marnie Smith. How is my son?"

"Not good. His fever is over one hundred and four degrees and rising. We have to get his fever down or I'm afraid Billy might have permanent brain damage," said Dr. Stevens.

"What can I do?" asked Marnie.

"Pray. Billy will have to stay with us until his fever is under control," said Dr. Stevens.

"What is wrong with my son?" Is his fever caused by his infection?" asked Marnie.

"I believe it is. But I won't know for sure until I can run some blood tests. Mrs. Smith, you might as well go home and get some rest. We will keep a close eye on your son to make sure he has the best care possible. Don't worry, he'll be all right," said Dr. Stevens.

"Thank you, Dr. Stevens. You have my telephone number if you need to get a hold of me," said Marnie. Then she and Mr. Boyagian left the hospital to return home.

Marnie cried all the way home. She couldn't control her emotions. This was her only son and she was very worried about his safety. She felt bad that she couldn't help him out of this terrible situation.

Mr. Boyagian dropped Marnie off in front of her house, but before leaving he tried to console her.

"Be strong, Marnie, for Billy's sake. Don't worry, he'll be all right," said Mr. Boyagian.

"Thank you for everything, Mr. Boyagian. I don't know what I'd do without you," said Marnie, shutting the passenger door.

Marnie entered her home and began crying once again. But she soon realized crying didn't help. It only made things worse. In order to take her mind off her son's problems, she began doing household chores. She cleaned the house from top to bottom until she was too tired to do any more. She finally went to bed at two o'clock in the morning. She had worked so hard that she fell asleep as soon as her head hit the pillow.

However, after only a few hours of sleep, the loud ringing of the telephone awakened Marnie. With her eyes still closed, she reached out and grabbed the phone.

"Hello."

"Mrs. Smith? This is Doctor Stevens. I would like you to come down to the hospital as soon as possible. Billy's condition has taken a turn for the worse," said Dr. Stevens.

"What's wrong?" asked Marnie as she jumped out of bed and paced the room, waiting for an answer.

"I don't want to tell you over the phone. I'll speak with you when you arrive at the hospital," said Dr. Stevens.

When the phone conversation with Dr. Stevens had ended, Marnie phoned her dear friend, Mr. Boyagian, hoping he could drive her to the hospital.

Once Marnie explained the emergency situation to Mr. Boyagian, he quickly agreed to help her. Two minutes later, he was waiting for her in front of her house.

Marnie ran out of her house as soon as Mr. Boyagian had honked his horn. The second she entered his car, she thanked him and began crying.

"It's all right to cry, Marnie. Let it out. But you must be strong at the hospital. Billy depends on your strength," said Mr. Boyagian.

Within five minutes, they were in the hospital emergency room waiting to speak with Dr. Stevens. The first time Marnie called out the doctor's name, he was there to meet her.

"Mrs. Smith, would you please come with me?" asked Dr. Stevens. He escorted her and Mr. Boyagian to a small room where she saw her unconscious son immersed in a bathtub full of ice cubes.

Marnie stood in stunned silence and disbelief as she watched two nurses adding more and more buckets of ice cubes to her son's bath. They nearly overflowed onto the floor.

"Dr. Stevens, what are you doing to my son?" asked Marnie.

"We're trying desperately to bring down your son's fever, which we believe is partially responsible for your son being in a coma," said Dr. Stevens.

"Oh no. What do you mean my son's in a coma? How did this happen?" cried Marnie.

"Once I reviewed Billy's CAT scan and blood tests, we located a blood clot that was pressing on a main artery in his brain. We were able to dissolve it with the use of anti-clotting medicine but the fever remained. While we were combating both problems, Billy suddenly lapsed into a coma," said Dr. Stevens.

"Will my son come out of it?" asked Marnie, as Mr. Boyagian consoled her.

"We certainly hope so. We've cleaned up his infection and dissolved his blood clot. I'm hoping once we get the fever down that he will come out of it," said Dr. Stevens.

After lying in ice for more than two hours, Billy's fever stabilized and slowly began coming down. Though he remained in a coma, he was still breathing on his own, which was a good sign and a good reason not to give up hope.

Mr. Boyagian had to leave Marnie at the hospital so he could return to his daily duties at the pet shop. But he returned to the hospital an hour before closing time so he could give Marnie a ride home and to see how little Billy was getting along. He saw Marnie in the waiting room pacing back and forth.

"Marnie, how's Billy doing? Has there been any change in his condition since this morning?" asked Mr. Boyagian.

"I don't know. I haven't heard anything since you left this morning," said a teary-eyed Marnie.

"You mean you've been waiting here all this time and nobody has come to speak with you about Billy's condition?" asked Mr. Boyagian.

"That's right. I was going to ask them but I didn't want to make a pest of myself," said Marnie.

Just then, a voice came over the hospital's intercom telling visitors that visiting hours were over. After nearly twelve hours of pacing and praying in Billy's hospital room, Marnie was forced to leave. However, before she left the hospital with Mr. Boyagian, Dr. Stevens came out and consoled her.

"Don't worry, Mrs. Smith. We'll take good care of Billy. I'll contact you as soon as there's a change in his condition," said Dr. Stevens.

"Dr. Stevens, please make my son healthy again," said Marnie as she turned and left the hospital with Mr. Boyagian.

Mr. Boyagian dropped Marnie off in front of her home. Before he parked his car, Mr. Boyagian watched her unlock her door and enter the house.

The minute Marnie entered her home she knelt down and prayed for the return of her son's health. Then she lay down on the couch and cried herself to sleep.

Over the next few days, Billy's condition stabilized and the hospital staff took him off of the critical list. Now they hoped he would come out of his coma. Though the doctor gave little hope for Billy's recovery, Marnie refused to give up on her son. She knew Billy was going to get better.

Every day after visiting her comatose son, Marnie would return home and go directly into Billy's room. She would walk to his bed, kneel down and pray that her son would come back home. She also prayed that her son's pet turtle would get well too.

Since Ned October had been injured, he hadn't moved out of his shell. Marnie thought he was dead. But while she was praying next to Billy's bed, her thoughts were interrupted when she thought she heard a ruffling noise coming from Billy's bedside table. She thought for a split second that the toy soldiers surrounding Billy's pet turtle were marching around Ned's turtle bowl. But when she looked more closely, she knew that her eyes had been playing tricks on her.

Marnie returned to her praying but again her thoughts were interrupted by a ruffling noise coming from Billy's bedside table. When she stood to see where the noise was coming from, she was surprised to see Ned moving around on the gravel surrounding his little island. That was the ruffling noise Marnie had heard. She was so happy that Ned had come out of his shell that she began to cry.

At that moment, Billy's mother thought that maybe her son had also come out of his coma. So she phoned the hospital to find out the condition of her son's illness. Marnie was told, however, that there had been no improvement and her son was still in his coma. She became even more depressed and sad. After praying for her son's recovery, she cried herself to sleep on his bed.

Marnie refused to give up, however. She would do whatever it took to wake her son out of his coma. She knew how Billy had loved his pet turtle, Ned October, so she had an idea. She decided to bring Ned with her to the hospital to visit Billy, hoping that he would have a comforting effect on her son. But deep down in her heart, she didn't expect anything to happen but she hoped this would be the answer to her prayers. She really needed a miracle.

Marnie phoned Mr. Boyagian and asked him for a ride to the hospital. He happily obliged and was sitting in his car waiting for Marnie in front of her house less than two minutes later. But he was a little perplexed when he saw her carrying the small cardboard case.

"What's in the case?" asked Mr. Boyagian as Marnie opened the passenger door and got into the car.

"I'm taking Billy's pet turtle to the hospital with me," said Marnie.

"Is it dead or alive?" asked Mr. Boyagian.

"Ned's alive. He finally came out of his coma. I'm hoping Billy will too when he senses Ned's presence," said Marnie.

"I hope so too. I'm just glad Ned didn't die from shell shock," said Mr. Boyagian as he entered the hospital parking lot.

Mr. Boyagian dropped Marnie off in front of the hospital then drove to his pet store. He promised to return later that evening.

Marnie was anxious to see her son, hoping that he would react to the surprise she had in store for him. When she entered Billy's room, Marnie went to stand next to his bed to kiss him on his cheek. When she straightened up, she undid the top of Ned's small carrying case and lifted him out of the box. Marnie then called out to her son.

"Billy, look who came to see you. It's Ned October. He finally came out of his shell just to visit you. Look honey, Ned's here," said Marnie. She held Ned in her hand in front of Billy's little unconscious face, hoping for some kind of reaction.

When Billy didn't react to Ned, his mother started to return Ned to his carrying case, but then she had another thought. Marnie decided to let Ned crawl on her son's chest, just as her son had let him do many times before. Marnie hoped that her son might feel the movement of the turtle's little feet and awaken from his coma.

As Marnie placed Ned on her son's chest, she knelt down alongside the bed and began praying for her son's recovery. But after a few minutes of prayer, she decided that it was a bad idea and nothing was going to come of it. She reached out to grab the turtle to return him to his carrying case, when all of a sudden she noticed her son's eyes open. But then they closed again.

Marnie quickly picked up Ned October and placed him in his carrying case. Then she watched her son's face to see if he would respond to her voice.

"Billy, Mommy's here. Ned October's here too," she said.

At that moment, Billy opened up his eyes and looked right into his mother's eyes.

"Mom, where am I?" asked little Billy.

"Oh my little love, you are all right," cried Marnie as she squeezed her son's hand in hers.

"You said Ned is here. Where is my turtle?" asked Billy.

"Here he is. I have him," said Marnie. She lifted Ned out of his case and set him on her son's chest.

Billy picked up his little friend and held him in his hand. He lifted Ned up to his mouth and gave him a little kiss on his head. Then he placed Ned onto his chest and let him run rampant.

While Billy was playing and talking with his pet turtle, his mother was thanking the heavens above for her son's recovery. At that moment, a nurse came running into the room to see what all the commotion was about. She was surprised and flabbergasted to see the little boy wide-awake and talking coherently to a little, green turtle.

Dr. Stevens was called into the room to check the status of Billy's illness.

"Does anyone know what made Billy awaken?" asked Dr. Stevens.

"I think the bond between my son and his pet turtle, Ned October, was the reason my son came out of his coma. The minute my son felt Ned crawling around on his chest, he opened his eyes," said Marnie.

"I don't know if Billy's pet turtle had anything to do with him awakening or not, but whatever happened, it was a miracle," said Dr. Stevens.

"Yeah, a miracle named Ned October," said Marnie. She stood back then as Dr. Stevens tested Billy's reflexes.

After preliminary tests had been completed, Billy was given an incredible clean bill of health. However, he would have to stay in the hospital until Dr. Stevens could go over Billy's blood tests. If the test results proved to be normal, Billy would be released from the hospital and allowed to go home.

Twelve hours after Billy had awakened from his coma he was allowed to leave the hospital. Mr. Boyagian, as he had promised, was at the hospital just before the close of visiting hours. He was very surprised and happy to see that Billy had come out of his coma and had been given a clean bill of health.

"Marnie, this is a miracle," said a smiling Mr. Boyagian.

"You can say that again," responded the nurse.

"Marnie, did you show Billy his pet turtle?" asked Mr. Boyagian.

The second Billy heard Mr. Boyagian talking about his pet turtle, he held up his little, green friend to show everyone.

"Ned October is right here with me," said Billy as his mother began helping him get dressed.

"I believe Ned is the reason Billy came out of his coma. When Billy felt Ned's footsteps on his chest, he suddenly woke up," said Marnie, affectionately rubbing her son's shoulders.

Once Billy was dressed, he and his little friend, Ned, were placed into a wheelchair and wheeled out of the hospital to Mr.

Boyagian's waiting car. Many of the hospital staff that had cared for Billy came along to say goodbye as Billy, his mother, Ned, and Mr. Boyagian loaded themselves into the car and drove away.

Mr. Boyagian drove Billy and his mother back home and helped them out of the car and into their house. He was a very caring neighbor and friend and wanted the best for his next-door neighbors.

"Marnie, if you need me for anything, I'm just a phone call away," said Mr. Boyagian.

"Thank you for everything, Mr. Boyagian. I don't know what I would have done without you," said Marnie as she gave him a kiss on the cheek.

Mr. Boyagian became embarrassed and walked out the front door to return to his home, while Marnie and her son tried to get back to a normal life.

Chapter 5

Five days after Billy arrived home from the hospital he was as healthy as he was before the accident. He was his old, energetic self and bided his time between home studies with his tutor and playing with Ned October. Billy and Ned were happy once again. They had both kicked their comas to the curb. However, their troubles were not yet over.

The day had come when Ned's home needed to be cleaned. It had been over two weeks since Billy had purchased Ned and his bowl hadn't been cleaned since Billy's illness. But Billy had promised his mother that he would clean Ned's home at least once every two weeks and the time had come to keep his promise.

Billy picked up Ned and his turtle bowl and headed for the bathroom where he would clean the bowl. First, he grabbed Ned and placed him into the clean toilet water and let him swim while he cleaned out the bowl in the sink. Billy placed the bowl and its contents into the sink and began filling it with hot water.

When the bowl was half full with clean, hot water, Billy noticed that he had forgotten the cleaning rag. He quickly shut off the water and hurried to his room to fetch it.

But while Billy was out of the bathroom, his mother walked in not noticing the turtle bowl in the sink or the turtle in the toilet. After sneezing, Marnie wiped her nose with a Kleenex, threw it into the toilet, and then flushed it, ignorant of Ned's whereabouts or the chore that her son had been in the process of doing. She didn't notice Ned swirling around and around in the water before being sucked down into the city's deep, dark web of underground sewers.

After Billy's mother flushed the toilet, she returned to the living room, immune to the problems she had just caused.

When Billy returned to the bathroom with the cleaning rag, he didn't notice that Ned had disappeared until he finished cleaning the turtle bowl. Before calling to his mother, Billy looked all over the bathroom for his beloved pet. But when he realized that Ned was missing, he became very upset.

"Mom, Ned is missing. Do you know where he is?" asked Billy, as he ran to the living room to confront his mother.

"No. Isn't he in your room sleeping in his turtle bowl?" she asked.

"No. I had him in the toilet while I cleaned out his bowl. But I had to leave the bathroom to get a rag and when I returned, I cleaned the bowl and then reached into the toilet so I could put Ned back into his bowl but he was gone. Mom, did you take Ned out of the toilet?" asked Billy.

"Honey, I flushed the toilet just a few minutes ago, but I would have noticed your turtle if he had been in there," she said.

"Mom, how could you! Ned was in there. You flushed Ned down the toilet. Now I'll never see him again. You killed my Ned October. He was the only friend I had in the whole world," whined Billy.

"I'm sorry honey. But I'm sure we'll find him. If not, we'll get you another turtle," she said.

"I don't want another turtle. I want Ned," cried Billy as he stomped his feet on the floor.

"Maybe Ned climbed out of the toilet before it was flushed and is still somewhere in the house. If that's the case, I'm sure we'll find him," said Marnie.

"How?" asked Billy.

"We'll have to search the house from top to bottom," said Marnie.

"What if we still don't find him?" asked Billy.

"Please honey, we'll worry about that bridge when we cross it," said Marnie.

"Where should I start looking?" asked Billy.

"Why don't you start in the bathroom and then, if you don't find him there, try your bedroom. I'll look in the hallway and living room," said Marnie.

As Billy scoured the house looking for his little pet turtle, Ned October was swirling through a long, dark corridor of dizzying, intertwining sewer pipes. Some of them were so tiny that Ned nearly got his small, round body hung up in them until a gushing flow of fresh toilet water tore him from the grasp of the sewer pipe.

After traveling through more than three-hundred feet of dirty, wet and smelly sewer pipes, Ned's journey finally came to an end. He was spit ten feet into the air and then fell hard into a large pool of smelly, polluted water. When he finally landed, he was completely disoriented. His surroundings in the underground sewers were so dark that all he could see was the whites of a predator's eyes that were lurking about for some unsuspecting, young, naïve prey to fill his empty stomach. Ned October was the perfect target.

When Ned was finally able to comprehend what had happened to him he became concerned and worried, not for his own life, but for that of his little friend's life. Ned tried calling out to him.

"Where are you, Billy? Help me. Help me, Billy," cried Ned October.

But something was wrong. Ned's voice had deteriorated due to his long illness from shell shock and it never returned. Just then Ned thought he had heard the cries of his little friend Billy way off in the distance.

"Ned, where are you? Come back, Ned," sobbed Billy.

"Don't cry Billy. I'll find you," cried Ned.

Ned wasn't sure if he heard Billy or not, but that wasn't going to stop him from finding his friend. Billy was his best and only friend. Ned decided never to give up until he was back home in his turtle bowl sitting next to Billy's bed.

So Ned set out to find his way back to his warm and cozy home. He missed his home and his only friend. After his parents abandoned Ned, he was left to fend for himself. Eventually he was taken to Mr. Boyagian's shop and adopted by Billy. Now Billy was Ned's hero.

But as Ned looked down the big, dark, winding corridor, he wondered when and where he would come out. He had no idea how long it would take to reach dry land, or daylight for that matter, and the water in the sewer was so deep that he had to swim with no place to rest.

Ned tried holding onto the side of the sewer for a second or two, but a large stream of rushing water drove him away. He was pushed into the center of the large sewer where he would either have to swim or float for hours at a time.

When Ned thought about the predicament he was in, he believed more and more that he had been purposely sent to this bad place. Being lost in a deep, dark cavern of never-ending, criss-crossing, intertwining sewer pipes was Ned's worst nightmare.

After floating and swimming for more than six hours through this dense jungle, Ned's fears magnified. He heard flapping sounds in the pitch black and then felt ripples of water slap against his face and shell as something from high above swooped down and snatched something out of the water right next to him.

Ned began swimming as fast as he could. He felt something hit the back of his shell, knocking him underwater. Ned couldn't see the evil demon stalking him from above, which made him even more frightened. So Ned swam underwater for a time hoping to get away from the predator that had been attacking him. By the time Ned had surfaced, his tormentor had disappeared and the attacks from above had subsided.

When Ned came up for air, he was breathing hard and exhausted. He checked out his dark surroundings and thought he saw a flash of light a few yards away. So he gathered up all his energy and strength and fought on, never giving up hope of finding his way back home. As Ned got closer to the twinkling light, he heard tinkling sounds. He believed he had found his way to daylight and was near the end of his long, lonesome journey. When he finally reached it however, he saw that it was only the sunlight coming through a sewer drain cover.

Ned was heartbroken and disappointed that the light didn't lead him to the freedom he sought. Instead he was still trapped in this huge, dark, smelly tunnel of the unknown.

Suddenly, marble-sized, red-hot charcoal ashes that someone from above had thrown through the sewer drain cover overwhelmed Ned. They came crashing down onto Ned's shell, knocking him out for just a nano-second. But quick thinking saved his life.

Diving deep into the polluted sewer water, Ned luckily dodged the multitude of fireballs, but was slightly injured while swimming for his life. Besides being struck by one of the red-hot coals, Ned also strained his leg muscles as he plunged his body into the depths of the bottomless pit.

Ned could only stay under for a few seconds at a time because the water was so full of toxic chemicals that it was almost impossible to stay underwater for any longer than that. But Ned fought his way out of this life-threatening situation, only to find himself facing death's door once again.

Just as Ned dodged the red-hot coals, another source of pollutants came crashing through the sewer drain. This time it was a waterfall of paint cleaners that came tumbling down on top of him, nearly drowning him. Ned had to ride this wave of deadly chemicals using his shell as a surfboard.

At that moment, Ned was a surfer. But his shell was starting to smoke and burn as the toxic chemicals began eating away at it. He decided that he needed to get away from the wave of death or he would be added to the pollutants in the sewer water.

At the last moment, Ned passed a couple of adjacent sewer pipes and was able to grab hold of the wall of one of the many intersecting pipes and crawl to safety. But he had a decision to make – either return to the big sewer and hope the toxic chemicals had passed, or follow this new tunnel and hope it would lead to a better place and put an end to his befuddled journey.

The pipe that Ned chose was very small compared to the sewer he had just escaped from. This one was only four inches round and went on forever. He couldn't see any light at the end of the tunnel. But Ned kept slowly inching forward, never giving up hope of finding his way home.

The only thing that Ned liked about this sewer pipe was that it was dry and warm. He crawled and crawled for so long that his aching, little feet had become sore and raw. But he still refused to give up. He continued to push forward, never giving up on his quest to find his home and to be reunited with his best friend, Billy.

After many long hours of endless silence, Ned became tired, hungry, weak, and thirsty. He needed to rest for a few minutes. But while Ned way lying on his back, up against the wall of the sewer pipe, he heard two loud thuds, then suddenly felt a rumbling beneath his feet. When he looked out into the blackness, he saw the whites of four big eyes staring down at him.

Suddenly, something knocked Ned from his comfortable position and pounced onto his back. Ned quickly retreated into his shell not wanting to end up on a predator's dining room table for dessert. But just a second before he retreated to safety, he felt one of his predator's fur coats. Ned believed that two large sewer rats were accosting him.

Ned soon felt himself being dragged sideways as this large, atrocious vermin grabbed him and then picked him up with his big, powerful jaws, nearly crushing his shell with his buckteeth. Somehow, Ned managed to hang on and push the pain out of his mind as he held on for dear life, wondering how he would get out of this mess. He was being kidnapped and taken for dinner to his captor's home. Ned felt his tortured body being lifted and bumped as his attacker entered his abode.

Finally, Ned's captor released his hold on Ned and dropped him into a nest full of baby rats. They were curious about the meal that their parent had brought for them to feast upon. But as the baby rats sniffed and gnawed at Ned's shell, Ned refused to come out and say "hello." Ned was busy trying to figure out how to escape from his furry captors.

Just then the other dirty rat in Ned's kidnapping came in to his friend's home and the two furry rodents began to argue. As far as Ned could ascertain, the two vermin were arguing over his demise. They refused to compromise and failed to come to an agreement because Ned's captor didn't want to give up any of his find.

Silence ensued and the two furry friends began fighting, while the baby rats returned to their room and hid under their soft beds. The two grown-ups continued fighting and acting like fools. Suddenly, Ned saw his opening. This was his chance to escape.

While his two kidnappers were locked in a wrestling hold, Ned came out of hiding and ran for his life. Within ten minutes he had fled his captor's home. Though he fell down the same four-inch round pipe that he had been in just before his kidnapping, Ned hurriedly plowed ahead, never looking back. He continued his long journey homeward hoping to be reunited one day with his one and only friend, Billy.

Chapter 6

While Ned wandered through the sewer pipe worrying about Billy, Billy frantically searched the house looking for Ned, unaware that he was lost. He looked all over the house, as did his mother, but they were unable to find poor, little Ned.

Since the disappearance of Billy's pet turtle, he had begun acting obnoxious and displaying troubled behavior. He acted like a spoiled brat. He blamed his mother for his missing turtle and started talking back to her, disrespecting her, and throwing temper tantrums to get his own way. Billy's mother was very disheartened and disturbed by his poor behavior. She was concerned by his behavior change and his continued obsession with his lost pet turtle, Ned October.

However, Marnie believed her son's dismal attitude and bad behavior was her fault because she had failed to be strict. She had never disciplined Billy before and now that lack of discipline came back to haunt her. Despite the lack of discipline, Billy was a good child and since Ned's arrival had become more attentive to his mother's wishes. However, since Ned's disappearance Billy had retreated to his old ways and his mother was at her wits' end.

When little Billy returned to his room for some much-needed rest, his mother called her good friend and next-door neighbor.

"Hello, Mr. Boyagian, this is Marnie. I hate to disturb you, but I need your help."

"Yes, Marnie. What can I do for you?" he asked.

"My son is so heartbroken over the loss of his pet turtle that I would like to replace it with another one. Can you bring me a turtle that looks exactly like Ned? But Billy mustn't know about this. I want to surprise him," said Marnie.

"You're not going to tell him that the replacement turtle is Ned, are you?" asked Mr. Boyagian.

"Yes, that was my plan. He's constantly looking around the house hoping that he'll find Ned. But I know deep down in my heart that I flushed him down the toilet. Billy won't be the same until Ned is back," said Marnie.

"Marnie, I don't think you should try and fool your son like that. But I'm willing to help you. I just hope you know what you're doing," said Mr. Boyagian.

"So do I. I know it's not right to fool him but I'm doing it out of love. He's feeling so low and depressed that I will do anything to make him happy. I'm sure he'll never know the difference between Ned and the new turtle. They all look alike," she said.

"Yes they do look alike. I just hope your son doesn't see a difference. But I'll do as you ask. Billy deserves to be happy," said Mr. Boyagian.

"Thank you, Mr. Boyagian. When can you bring the turtle over?" asked Marnie.

"I will drop one off on my way home from the pet shop. I just ask that you don't tell Billy that I was involved in your little scheme. Especially if he finds out that you lied to him. Do we have a deal?" asked Mr. Boyagian.

"Yes. We have a deal. I promise I won't mention your name," said Marnie.

While Marnie was waiting for Mr. Boyagian to arrive with Ned's replacement, Billy was supposed to be in his bedroom taking a nap, but he had another idea in mind. Billy placed Ned's bowl on the floor then placed a little wooden ramp leading from the floor up to its lip. It was made so Ned could crawl back into his home without anyone's help, especially if Billy was sleeping or out of the room. Billy was certain Ned would find his way to the bedroom and return to his bowl.

When Billy was satisfied that his chore was completed, he hopped into bed for a quick nap. He hadn't slept well since Ned had been gone. As soon as his head hit the pillow, he was sound asleep. He stayed that way for nearly two hours.

The second Billy opened his eyes, he slid across his bed to see if Ned had found his way home but was disappointed that the bowl was still empty. Billy jumped out of bed and went into the living room to talk to his mother about Ned's disappearance. He had been gone for nearly seven days and Billy was certain that Ned wasn't anywhere in the house. He now believed that Ned had been flushed down the toilet.

"Mom, I've looked for a week now and I can't find Ned anywhere. Are you sure you didn't flush him down the toilet? If you did, I'm sure it was an accident. I know you didn't do it on purpose, did you?" asked Billy looking up directly into his mother's blue eyes.

"I'm sure I didn't. At least I hope I didn't. I still believe Ned will show up. He has to be around this house somewhere," said Marnie looking away from her son's glare.

"I'll keep looking if you think I'll find him. He's probably starving by now," said Billy as he walked back to his room.

Later that evening, while Billy was playing in his room, Mr. Boyagian finally came over carrying a small, white, cardboard case that contained a Ned look-alike. Marnie just hoped Billy would believe this replacement was Ned.

Mr. Boyagian handed the case containing the turtle to Marnie. "Here's your turtle. I hope you can pull it off," he said.

"Would you like to come in, Mr. Boyagian?" asked Marnie.

"No. I don't want to be around when you tell Billy that you found Ned. He's much smarter than you realize," said Mr. Boyagian.

Marnie shut her front door after Mr. Boyagian left and quietly walked into the kitchen to hide the new turtle until she could decide her next move. She took the turtle out of the case, placed it into the sink, and crushed and discarded the case in the garbage to get rid of the evidence. Then she sat for a minute to calm her nerves and gather enough strength to put her next move into motion. She had to find the perfect hiding place – a place where her son hadn't looked yet.

Marnie knew that she wasn't being truthful but she wanted to bring her son back to reality. After Ned October had helped Billy recover from his illness, he was a happy child. But now he was reverting back to his old behavior. Billy was so obsessed with Ned that Marnie had no other recourse but to put her plan into action. What could she lose? If her son fell for it, great, if not, then she would have to think of something else.

The Hunt for Ned October

Marnie wanted to get her son's mind off of Ned and back onto his studies because he had to return to school. She took three deep breaths, picked up the little turtle from the sink and walked into the living room. She looked for a place where Billy wouldn't have searched. She found a little spot in a far off corner of a hall closet, adjacent to the bathroom. This would have been a perfect spot for Ned to get lost in so she set Ned's replacement there and placed debris over him, partially covering the little turtle's shell.

Marnie was about to put the second stage of her plan into motion. After she said a quick prayer and took another three deep breaths, she called out to her son.

"Billy, come here, quick. I want you to see something. I think I've got good news for you," she said.

Billy opened his bedroom door and hurried to find his mother. He wondered what all the excitement was about.

"What do you want, Mom?" asked Billy as he stood near his mother.

"Look what I found," she said, pointing to the closet floor.

"What is it?" asked Billy. He knelt forward to see what his mother was pointing at.

"I think we've finally found Ned October," said Marnie as she picked up the turtle and handed it to her son.

Billy happily held the small, green turtle in his cupped hands looking over his little pal. He then hugged his mother with deep love in his heart.

"Thank you, Mom. I'm going to put Ned back into his turtle bowl and feed him. He hasn't eaten in a week. He must be starved," said Billy.

"Oh, he probably found some bugs to chew on while he was on the run," said Marnie.

Billy skipped back to his room with his little friend in tow, while his mother returned to the living room, happy that her plan had worked. Her son was happy again; the second he saw the little, green shell his face lit up like a thousand sparkles going off at once.

But Marnie's happiness was short lived. Ten minutes after finding the turtle, Billy knew that this turtle was not his Ned. So he carried it to the living room and confronted his mother.

"Mom, I don't know where this turtle came from, but it isn't Ned. This turtle is a female and should be called Nadene," said

Billy, holding the turtle close to his mother's eyes.

"Billy, how do you know that the turtle is a female?" she asked.

"This turtle has four more spots on her stomach than Ned had and it's got yellow ears. Ned's spots are different," said Billy.

"Then how did this turtle get here then?" asked Billy's mother.

"I don't know, but it's not Ned. I know you flushed Ned down the toilet into the sewers below. I just hope he's still alive and can find his way home," said Billy.

When Billy's mother broke down and began to cry, Billy consoled her.

"I'm sorry, honey. I just wanted to make you happy," she cried.

"I like the turtle, Mom. But that doesn't mean that I'm gonna give up the hunt for Ned October. I still believe in my heart that Ned is alive and well," said Billy.

Billy kissed his mother on the cheek and returned to his bedroom holding his new turtle in his hands. Ned would have a girlfriend waiting for him when he returned home.

CHAPTER 7

As Billy made friends with Nadene, his new pet turtle, Ned October was busy struggling to free himself from the dark sewers, which he thought of as a black cauldron of horror. Ned was still trapped in the smaller sewer drain but continued slowly forward hoping it would lead him to daylight and freedom.

Ned constantly cried out for his pal, Billy, but his silent whining only made him lonelier. He crawled along the dry sewer pipe praying that he would make it out alive. But suddenly, he heard what sounded like shuffling footsteps closing in on him from behind. Ned crawled as fast as he could, thinking the worst. The pitter-patter sounds came down on Ned like a rushing freight train.

When Ned turned his little head to see what made the sound, he suddenly saw the eyes of his predators. It was the two rats that had kidnapped him just hours before and tried to have him for dinner. Luckily he escaped their grasp before, but now he wasn't so sure he would be that lucky again.

Ned could feel his stalkers breath as their massive jaws snapped at his little tail trying to reel him in for a quick snack. Just then Ned saw light ahead and put his shell into fifth gear as the rats trampled each other trying to gain control of their prey. But Ned wondered if he could run fast enough to evade the grasp of the two ruddy rodents.

Just as Ned reached the light of salvation, he found himself falling into a cold, rushing pool of raw sewage. The two furry rodents fell close behind.

When Ned surfaced, he was attacked from above by a flock of hungry bats and from behind by the predators that had forced him into his present unhealthy situation. The rats attacked first. They circled him and then began pouncing on poor Ned. Then the bats swooped down upon Ned hoping to catch their dinner. But instead of catching Ned, the bats scooped up the rats, inadvertently saving Ned's young life.

Ned swam away through the thick, raw sewage as fast as he could, thinking that he was out of danger. But just as his tired body began to relax, more bats suddenly swooped down and pummeled Ned's shell until one of them picked him up and tried to fly away with him. But Ned reached out and grabbed a large branch that was half-emerged in the raw muck and sewage.

However, the bat battled Ned until Ned's little body could hold on no longer. He tried with one last burst of energy to hang onto the branch knowing his life was at stake, but he was exhausted from fleeing one predator after another. Finally, Ned let go of his safety net and began rising into the air, firmly clutched in the bat's jaws. But the end was not near for Ned. As the bat lifted his slick body and little Ned into the air, thinking that dinner would soon be on the table, he got the shock of his life.

A three-foot alligator had been watching and following Ned since he had fallen into the quagmire and raw sewage. He had been biding his time, waiting for the chance to fill his belly without too much of a fight. The alligator knew that the little turtle was in his domain where he had been king of this jungle ever since he had been flushed down the toilet nearly four years before, just as Ned had been.

As the bat began to rise into the dark, foul air with Ned in tow, the alligator leapt from his hiding spot and sucked the flying bat into his large, massive jaws, swallowing his prey in one gulp. In the meantime, Ned went flying through the air before finally crashing back into the raw sewage.

Ned flew more than ten feet before smashing into the same large branch that he had tried to hang on to for dear life. The sudden shock to his body was similar to the one he felt at Billy's house when he fell into a long coma. This incident left him unconscious and floating on top of the raw sewage all alone and a target for any other predators looking for a quick and easy snack.

While Ned laid unconscious, dead to the world, Billy was busy making friends with Nadene, his new turtle. But Billy hadn't forgotten about his buddy, Ned. He began making plans to expand his search from his home to the sewers of the city and other important areas that could yield a happy ending to his search for Ned October.

However, Billy and his mother were unaware that someone else was lurking in the shadows also searching for Ned October. They were no ordinary citizens though. In fact, they didn't even belong in the United States at all. They were the people who had been arrested at Mr. Boyagian's Pet and Toy Shop, but before they were taken into custody, they had injected a hi-tech computer chip into Ned's body so that they weren't caught with it upon arrest.

The U.S. government agents weren't aware of this though. The chip contained the codes for the United States' chemical, biological, and nuclear arsenal, along with the plans, blueprints, and software that outlined the missile defense system of the entire nation. After injecting the turtle, they placed it amongst more than one hundred other small, green turtles hoping to retrieve the turtle and microchip at a later date and return to their native country as heroes.

The spies had been released due to a lack of evidence, and they were now searching high and low for the turtle that contained the United States' important secrets.

They had returned to Mr. Boyagian's Pet and Toy Shop and purchased every small, green turtle in the shop but were disappointed to learn that their microchip wasn't among the hundred or so turtles that they had taken back to their residence and x-rayed using a miniature fluoroscope. If they returned to their country without this important information contained on the computer chip, the very people that had sent them to the United States would execute them.

Once the spies had learned that their microchip wasn't in any of the turtles that they had just purchased, they quickly returned to Mr. Boyagian's shop. They confronted Mr. Boyagian and ordered him to turn over any and every receipt from the customers that had purchased a turtle from the day the government agents had arrested them to the present.

Upon being threatened by the criminal thugs, Mr. Boyagian handed over the receipts, which included the names and addresses of many of his friends and neighbors, including Billy Smith. He had given them a list of more than twenty-five customers that had purchased a pet turtle over the last few weeks. Now the spies had to sort out the list and find the turtle in question. Hopefully, they could do so without using any type of violence.

The Russian spies left Mr. Boyagian's Pet Shop to figure out their next step in tracking down their prey. Meanwhile, Billy was busy speaking with his mother about his plans to find his buddy, Ned October.

Mr. Boyagian knew it was wrong but never contacted any of the people about giving their addresses to the two thugs because he didn't want to worry them, especially little Billy and his mother because of all the heartache that had descended upon them of late.

Billy and his mother weren't aware of the trouble that had happened at the pet shop. Even though they had caught a glimpse of the large crowd of law enforcement officials exiting the pet shop that day, they never thought anything about it. They would soon find out differently though.

But in the meantime, Billy badgered his mother for help in making up flyers to place all around town asking for any information and offering a small reward leading to the whereabouts and/or return of Ned October.

"Mom, I need your help. Will you help me?" asked Billy.

"What do you need, honey?" she asked.

"I want to make up some posters with Ned's picture on them and put them up all over town. Then I'm going to broaden my search to the city's sewers and I won't stop looking until I find Ned," said Billy.

"Honey, I know you loved Ned, but you must realize that he might never come home. I thought you would have turned your attention to your new turtle by now. Ned's been gone for nearly two weeks already," said Marnie.

"I like Nadene, but I want Ned back. He's my best friend. I won't give up my search until I find him. Please help me make up some posters. I broke open my piggy bank and counted over twenty-six dollars that I can use as a reward for information leading to Ned's return," said Billy.

"Billy, I'm surprised at you. You were saving that money for something special," said Marnie.

"But Ned needs it more. I have plenty of time to save money for college. But now I'll use it for a reward," said Billy.

"Okay, I'll help you even though I don't know how I'm going to pay this hospital bill. I'll ask Mr. Boyagian to make up some flyers on his computer printer. I'm sure he'll help us. He always has before," said Marnie.

"Mom, I thought I might even ask our local police and fire departments to help in my search," said Billy.

"Don't be silly, Billy. They won't help you. They can't. They're too busy with the city's troubles. They don't have time to look for your pet turtle. You should ask Tommy and the neighborhood kids to help you look for Ned," she said.

"I don't think Tommy likes me. But I'll ask him to help me anyway. Maybe he can help me search the city's sewers," said Billy.

"Billy, I don't want you near those sewers. They are too dangerous. You must promise me that you won't go near those sewers. Promise me," said Marnie.

Without his mother noticing, Billy crossed his fingers behind his back and said, "I promise."

Billy returned to his room to make plans to find Ned. In the meantime, his mother telephoned Mr. Boyagian asking him to help make the flyers for her son. Mr. Boyagian agreed to help and promised to deliver nearly one-hundred flyers to her house with Ned's picture on them, offering a reward for any information leading to Ned October's return. They were delivered to the house two days later.

CHAPTER 8

While Billy was in his bedroom strategizing, Ned was still floating unconsciously on his back. The three-foot alligator that had tried to capture Ned earlier was now slowly crawling Ned's way. But neither Billy nor Ned was aware of the two Russian spies that were tracking down the addresses on the list Mr. Boyagian had given them.

Using a miniature fluoroscope, the spies would be able to x-ray each turtle and within minutes see if their microchip was hidden inside the turtle's body. With this type of equipment, they could break into the turtle's residence and not leave any trace of their having been there.

Using their numerous connections, the Russian spies were able to borrow a Fish and Game vehicle, clothing, and identification that named them as U.S. Fish and Game officials and hoped that this ruse would get them into the turtle owners' residences without casting suspicion upon themselves.

The spies had worked out a plan. They would tell the homeowners in question that the turtles they had recently purchased may be infected with a rare disease and that by using their miniature fluoroscope they would be able to tell if the turtle was diseased or not without putting it through any type of trauma.

The first address the Russian spies tracked down was a small, two-bedroom home only three blocks from Billy's house. Within a few minutes, they were knocking at the front door hoping to find their precious prize turtle. A woman in her mid-thirties opened it.

"Yes, may I help you?" asked the homeowner.

The spies showed the lady their phony Fish and Game identification. "Hello. We are Fish and Game inspectors. I'm Inspector

Tell and this beautiful lady is Inspector Moore. We have reason to believe that you purchased two small, green turtles from Mr. Boyagian's Pet and Toy Shop a few weeks ago. Is that true?" he asked.

"Yes. My two sons each bought a pet turtle. Why?" asked the homeowner.

"We believe that your pet turtles might have a contagious disease and we need to check them with our miniature fluoroscope. We promise not to harm them in any way and it will only take a few seconds to check them out. Then we'll be on our way," said Inspector Tell.

"What if you find out that the turtles have this contagious disease? What will happen to them?" asked the woman.

"We'll have to take them with us to be destroyed. We won't know if they have contaminated your family until their autopsies are completed," said Inspector Tell.

"Please, come in. I'll show you where the turtles are," said the homeowner as she escorted the two spies into her boys' bedroom.

One spy held onto the turtle while the other held the fluoroscope to its body. Within a few minutes, both turtles had been checked and were found to be free of the important microchip that the two Russian spies were looking for.

"Ma'am, your turtles are free of disease so we can give them our seal of approval. Now we'll get out of your hair. We thank you for your time and cooperation," said Inspector Tell.

The two spies left the woman's home and began searching for the second address on their list. The next owner had also purchased two turtles from Mr. Boyagian's shop within the past two weeks. The owner wasn't home, but that didn't stop them from completing their task. They easily broke into the home and searched out the turtles in question. Again, after x-raying the two turtles with the miniature fluoroscope, the two spies found them to be free of the microchip as well. They were in and out of the house within five minutes without anyone being the wiser.

The spies continued their search for the turtle. They would visit twenty-three homes within seven days before finally reaching Billy's residence to see if his turtle was the one with the imbedded microchip.

But in the meantime, Billy was gathering the utensils and tools that were needed to fasten the flyers to telephone poles and other places around the city. He hoped it would encourage the city's citizens to get involved in the hunt for Ned October.

As Billy was busy doing his chores to bring Ned home safe and sound, Ned was just waking up after having been knocked unconscious. A few seconds after Ned came back to reality he dusted the cobwebs out of his head as his eyesight finally returned to normal. But as his eyes adjusted to the darkness around him, he was soon confronted with yet another obstacle that would try to thwart his escape to freedom. He saw the three-foot long alligator creeping slowly towards him.

After the alligator snacked on the low-flying bat, he went looking for more nutritious food. That's when he discovered Ned lying very still. The alligator crept up from behind and smelled his prey. Ned tried to flee but was frozen in place with fear. When he tried to run away, his legs refused the commands from his brain. But finally, after some coercing, Ned's feet began to move one step at a time. But the sneaky alligator continued stalking Ned until he got so close that Ned could feel his breath on the back of his shell. At that moment, Ned suddenly felt an empty void of worthlessness. For a split second Ned had the feeling that he would soon be the alligator's next meal.

As Ned ran for his life, the alligator continued to follow close behind. He was waiting for the right time to make his move and scoop Ned into his massive jaws, grinding him up into little pieces with his sharp teeth. But Ned had other ideas.

Ned sighted daylight more than fifty feet away and wondered if he would make it to freedom before the alligator had him for lunch. But Ned refused to give up hope. He suddenly felt a big surge of adrenaline and energy then charged up his afterburners.

Ned ran faster than he had ever run before, but the alligator continued to keep pace with him. Ned wouldn't give up though. He continued on, praying and hoping that he would again see his little friend, Billy. Then, when Ned was only a few feet away from the large opening of the sewer that would take him out of darkness and into the light, the alligator suddenly leapt out of the sewer's muck and dove for Ned to make a quick snack of him.

But Ned quickly ducked under a pile of rubble and stayed hidden until the alligator swatted away at Ned's hideout. Using one of his short, stubby hands, the alligator reached into the murky water searching for Ned, but was unable to locate him. When Ned surfaced for air, the alligator saw him and was perched for action. Ned stood frozen in time. He was too frightened to move, knowing his time had come and would soon be in turtle heaven.

Suddenly, Ned and the alligator felt a massive earthquake rumbling beneath their bodies. Then came loud, booming voices that sounded as though they were a mob of more than one hundred people. Once again, Ned was confronted with more adversaries.

Ned, however, wasn't the only frightened animal in the smelly sewer. The alligator, who was just seconds away from eating Ned for lunch, was even more frightened when he saw many young boys running and playing just feet away in the city's sewers.

The alligator quickly turned and dove into the murky water to get as far away from the humans as he could. But Ned very carefully dodged a plethora of trampling feet as best he could without getting smashed under them.

Ned thought his nightmare was finally over when the large group of young boys passed by. But the boys turned on their flashlights and lit up the darkened sewer.

Ned was blinded by the intense light and dove deep into the dirty, murky, sewer water. He wasn't sure if he had been seen or not. He decided to stay hidden in the water until the boys were far enough away that he could flee to safety and daylight.

While Ned hid on the bottom of the smelly sewer, he could see the bright light shining over him on top of the water. He thought his ploy had worked and he had escaped the boys' wrath, that is, until he saw several hands searching in the dirty sewer water close to his hiding place. Ned tried to escape their searching human hands as he had their human feet, but he had to come up for air. And when he did pop his head above the water, he was seen immediately by one of the young boys.

The second the boy saw Ned, he reached down and scooped up the little, green turtle into his small, smooth hands. As the young boys gathered around to see what their comrade had found, Ned retreated back into his shell and refused to come out. As his new owner tried to coax Ned out of his shell by shaking him, like a salt shaker, the other boys took turns as well. Each boy tried to get Ned out of his shell by hitting or shaking him. He was abused so much by the boys that Ned's body was one big bruise by the time he was given back to his new owner.

Then the boys began to argue over Ned. They all wanted to own him and each believed they had seen him first. But the boy who was lucky enough to have scooped Ned out of the water refused to give in to his playmates' demands and claimed Ned for himself.

However, within a few minutes, once the initial surprise wore off, the boys regressed back to their inquisitive nature. They again began searching the long and darkened cavern of the unknown hoping to discover its innermost secrets.

As the young boys began filing one-by-one deeper and deeper into the darkened sewer, Ned became a nuisance to his new owner and was placed into the boy's flannel shirt pocket. Ned stood up and scratched at the shirt pocket trying to rip it to shreds so he could escape his captor, but to no avail. He was entrenched in flannel that heated his little, green body to near boiling. But Ned soon felt a cool, windy breeze swirl around his shell helping extinguish his inner fire.

As the boy contemplated his next move, Ned was also trying to figure a way out of his current situation. As he thought about his future, Ned thought about his little friend, Billy, and the cool breeze and the sun's warm rays that comforted him.

Before these boys had captured him, Ned had hoped that Billy would be among this throng of boys. It wasn't to be. Ned ended up in a stranger's shirt pocket, not knowing what would happen next. Ned could only hope and pray his journey would have a safe and happy ending.

Once again, Ned felt a cool, windy breeze swirl around his little, green body and felt the sun's warm rays. He knew he was finally out of the sewers and into daylight. At first, it was a comforting feeling. But comfort turned into terror as the sun's rays became so hot that Ned thought he would soon be a roasted turtle.

Just when Ned thought he would be roasted alive, his captor suddenly pulled him out of his shirt pocket. Ned could feel the crisp, clean air on his body and prayed that freedom was nearby. But then, Ned's new owner began throwing him high into the air, nearly dropping him each time until he finally did fall into more dirty and polluted water. Ned quickly dove towards the bottom of this unfamiliar territory. He would soon learn that he had been thrown into a marsh just blocks away from his old homestead.

But the marsh was too polluted for him. Ned couldn't hold his breath any longer and had to come up for air. When he resurfaced, Ned's young kidnapper was leaning over him, waiting to snap him up. Ned again tried to swim away but this time he wasn't fast enough. His nemesis reached down and plucked Ned from the polluted water.

Ned's captor began telling the other boys that he was going to take his turtle home with him and keep him as a pet. That didn't set too well with the other boys and they began to argue as they did when they first found Ned in the sewer. The boys continued to bicker and argue over Ned's demise. He regressed back into his shell once again to keep himself invisible to the young boys' emotions.

As the boys began to fight and wrestle over ownership of the little, green turtle, poor Ned was getting the worst of it. He was nearly crushed in his captor's clasped hands as he tried to keep the other boys from getting their hands on his prize. But the boys were too rough and made Ned's captor squeal in pain.

Ned's new owner decided keeping Ned wasn't worth the trouble so he decided to get rid of the turtle. He figured if he couldn't have Ned, neither could the other boys. So with one big toss, Ned was thrown more than fifty feet into the air until he once again landed on his back inside the darkened, dreary sewer.

When Ned finally hit the water, he was knocked unconscious for nearly twenty minutes. Luckily, he was only ten feet away from the exit. So if and when Ned recuperated, he would only have a short way to crawl to freedom. Before that happened though, he would have another big obstacle to get through or somehow bypass – that was the marsh that he had been exposed to for a short time before he was thrown back into the darkened pit of no return.

CHAPTER 9

As Ned lay unconscious only feet away from the sewer's entrance, little Billy was getting ready to begin placing flyers all around town; but before Billy could leave the house his mother wanted to have a few words with him.

"Billy, I don't want you going near those sewers. Do you hear me?" asked Marnie.

"Yes, I hear you," he said.

"I don't want you to go alone. I want you to ask Tommy and the other neighborhood boys to tag along with you. Is that understood?" asked Marnie.

"But me and Tommy don't get along. And I don't know the other kids that well. I can hang the flyers without any help," said Billy.

"I don't care if you can or not. That's not the point. I don't want you walking around town alone. If you don't ask Tommy to go with you then I won't allow you to leave the house," said Marnie.

"Mom, I'm not a little kid anymore. I'm six and a half years old," said Billy.

"I know you're a big boy, Billy. But I'll worry about you if you go alone. You'll be safer if you have the other boys to tag along," said Marnie.

"Mom, I have never forgiven Tommy over that fight he and I had that caused Ned's injury," said Billy.

"Billy, sometimes you have to swallow your pride and compromise. It takes a bigger man to admit his mistake than run away from it," said Marnie.

"If you say so," sighed Billy.

"Why don't you go outside and ask Tommy if he wants to help you hang your flyers? I'm sure he'll want to help you find Ned October," said Marnie.

"Alright, if you insist. I'll ask him and a few of the other kids if they want to help me in my search for Ned October," said Billy.

"Good. Now I won't have to worry about you. But I want you home before dinner. Do you hear me, young man?" asked Marnie.

"I hear you, Mom," said Billy. He grabbed his flyers and tools then walked out the front door closing it behind him.

Billy stood on his porch watching Tommy and four of the neighborhood kids playing catch with a rubber ball.

"Hey, Tommy. Do you and the other guys want to help me hang flyers?" asked Billy, interrupting the boy's game.

"Hang flyers? For what?" asked Tommy.

"To find my pet turtle, Ned October. I'm offering a twenty-five dollar reward to anyone with information leading to the return of my turtle," said Billy as he showed Tommy and the other boys one of the flyers with Ned's picture on it.

"What happened to your pet turtle?" asked Jimmy, Tommy's younger brother.

"He was swept down the toilet into the sewers," said Billy.

"Billy, I thought you were mad at me. Didn't you say you would never play with me again?" asked Tommy.

"I know what I said. But I was wrong. I know now that Ned's injury was an accident and that you didn't do it on purpose," said Billy.

"I liked your turtle. I didn't mean to hurt him," said Tommy.

"I know. That's why I'm asking for your help. I want you to be my friend," said Billy.

"Billy, I've always been your friend. Sure, I'll help you with your flyers. So will Jimmy and the other guys. Just give us a few minutes so we can grab a hammer and some nails," said Tommy. He and other boys then ran to their homes to get the tools they would need to help Billy with his flyers.

Within a few minutes, Tommy and the rest of the boys returned with hammers hanging from their waists very anxious to start their work.

"Hey Billy, when do you want to start hanging flyers?" asked Jimmy.

"I want to wait until we get near the City Park," said Billy as they started walking towards the park that was more than six blocks away.

"Why wait? Let's hang them all over," said Tommy.

"I just don't want to waste any. I want to hang them where I think it will do the most good," said Billy.

"Whatever you say. You're the boss," said Tommy.

"Many of the sewer drains come out at the City Park. That's why I want to hang a lot of flyers in that area. In fact, maybe we'll get lucky and find Ned October swimming in the pond," said Billy.

"If Ned got sucked down the toilet into the sewers, why don't we search those sewer drains at the park?" asked Tommy.

"I can't. I'm not allowed to go near the sewers. My mom would punish me if she ever found out that I went into one of those sewer drains," said Billy.

"Jimmy and I aren't allowed to go near the sewer drains either. But if that's the only way for you to find your pet turtle, then take a chance and risk it. What my mother doesn't know won't hurt her," said Tommy.

"I don't know. I'll have to think about it. But if I do decide to go into the sewers will you guys follow me?" asked Billy.

"Yeah. We'll follow you, Billy," said the boys in unison.

The five boys continued walking towards the park anxious to begin hanging flyers in the hopes of rescuing Ned October. But they were afraid that Billy might never find his pet turtle even with his offer of a reward.

And they weren't aware of the Russian spies who had driven past them, looking for another address from their list, who were hoping to find the turtle that contained their precious microchip.

Unbeknownst to Billy, Ned October was more than four blocks away from the park and still lying unconscious in a bed of mucky, raw sewage. He was just a few feet away from the sewer drain's entrance where it dumped polluted contents into an automaker's industrial pond, very near its massive parking lot.

By the time Billy and his neighborhood friends reached the park's entrance, Ned was just emerging from his peaceful sleep. He opened up his little eyes and heard a faint rumbling far off in the distance until it built up to a loud roar. He could hear all the other trapped animals, amphibians, and mammals screaming for their lives until the sounds grew silent.

When Ned turned to see what all the commotion was about, he was confronted by a large wall of smelly sludge that was rolling as fast as the speed of sound. Ned held on for dear life as he was grabbed by a large wave of this murky, raw sewage and thrown through the air into the automaker's toxic, polluted pond that was used as a waste dump.

However, this time Ned wasn't knocked unconscious. He was only knocked out of breath after landing hard on his back in the murky depths of toxic horror. As in the sewer, this toxic waste was very detrimental to his health.

Within a few minutes of lying in the mucky waste, Ned's shell began to smolder and burn due to the toxicity of the pond water. As the toxic pollutants began to burn his little body, Ned quickly looked in all directions for the shortest possible route to safety. He needed a quick way out of this hostile environment before it swallowed him up.

Suddenly, a longhaired bumblebee flew just above Ned's head.

"Mr. Turtle, my name is Bobby Bee. Follow me and I'll lead you to safety," he said.

But Ned was up to his neck in sludge and could barely move. When Bobby Bee saw the trouble Ned was in, he flew in for a closer look.

"I can't, I'm stuck," said Ned.

"Mr. Turtle, grab on to my stinger and I'll pull you to land," said Bobby Bee. Ned grabbed onto his stinger as the bee slowly pulled him to safety.

"My name is Ned October. Thank you for your help. I couldn't have gotten out of there without it. You saved my life," whispered Ned, his voice barely audible.

"No thanks necessary, Ned. I'm glad I could help. But what's wrong with your voice?" asked Bobby Bee.

"I haven't been able to speak since an injury befell me a few weeks ago. But now my voice seems to be coming back," said Ned.

"What happened? How did you get injured?" asked Bobby Bee.

"My owner and his friend started wrestling and knocked over the table, which in turn, knocked me and my bowl to the floor. When I slammed into the floor, I was knocked unconscious and came to a few days later," said Ned.

"So what brings you to my side of town?" asked Bobby Bee.

"Luck, I think," said Ned.

"What do you mean?" asked Bobby Bee.

"I've been lost in the sewers for ages. I finally escaped its hold and ended up in this place. I don't know which is worse, the sewers or this waste dump," said Ned.

"If you had been in that sludge much longer, you'd have been smoked turtle," joked Bobby Bee.

"That's for sure. I don't know what that stuff is in that pond, but it's not water," said Ned.

"You got that right. So how did you end up in the city's sewers?" asked Bobby Bee.

"It's a long story," said Ned.

"I've got plenty of time," said Bobby Bee.

"Don't you have a family or wife to go home to?" asked Ned.

"No. But that's a long story too," said Bobby Bee.

"I've got plenty of time," said Ned, smiling.

"I'll make a deal with you. You tell me how you ended up in the sewers and I'll tell you my story. Is it a deal?" asked Bobby Bee, stroking his long, blond, shoulder-length hair.

"It's a deal. Well, one day my owner, Billy Smith, decided to clean my turtle bowl and placed me in the toilet bowl while he completed his task. The next thing I knew, I was suddenly swirling round and round the toilet bowl. Then, in a flash of an eye, I was swallowed up and flushed through a bunch of narrow pipes until I ended up in a big city sewer," said Ned.

"Boy. What a way to travel," said Bobby Bee.

"That's not the half of it. From the time I entered into the city's sewers, I was chased and stalked by some real evil predators. But luckily, I was able to dodge their grasp by going through a number of small and large sewer drains until I ended up in this one that whooshed me into this toxic pond. And in a nut shell, that's how I got here," said Ned.

"Boy, Ned, that's some story. You're lucky to be here at all. What kinds of predators were chasing you?" asked Bobby Bee.

"I'm not real sure. I've never seen anything like them before. I had some big, furry creatures capture me who were ready to have me for dinner but they began arguing and I was able to escape.

And then I was grabbed by some flying vampire and was in its clutches when all of a sudden another monster leapt into the air and snatched the winged creature, swallowing it whole," said Ned.

"How did you survive that?" asked Bobby Bee.

"Luckily, the flying vampire dropped me from its claws just as it was in the clutches of the monster's massive jaws. Somehow I was able to escape with my life in that incident too," said Ned.

"Boy, Ned. You have some story to tell. You should write a book about your adventures," said Bobby Bee.

"That's the kind of adventure I can do without," said Ned.

"Well, if you're rested up, I'll take you over and introduce you to the guys," said Bobby Bee.

"What guys?" asked Ned.

"Oh, it's just a bunch of us guys that have left home for one reason or another and now we're starting our own club of misfits. But they're all good guys. Come on and I'll let you meet them," said Bobby Bee, flying just above Ned who slowly crawled along, following him to his gang of misfits.

Just then, Ned heard a loud whistle.

"What's all that noise?" asked Ned.

"That's the automaker's whistle. It's time for the humans to change shifts," said Bobby Bee.

A few minutes later, Ned heard loud sounds that he wasn't familiar with. He heard car horns and people running to and fro and wondered what all the commotion was about. But Bobby Bee was used to it. He had heard it daily since he made the automaker's land his new home.

"Where are all those humans going?" asked Ned.

"Some are going home and some are going into the building to work. Don't worry about it. You'll soon get used to all the noise. Come on. We're almost at my friend's hangout. Just a few more yards to go," said Bobby Bee.

Within a few minutes, Bobby Bee was introducing Ned to all of his friends who were sitting and chatting around a little campfire made of broken matchsticks.

"Gather round, guys. I want you to meet a new friend of mine. This is Ned October. He was lost in the sewers and then thrown into the toxic pond. But I managed to save him and pull him to safety," said Bobby Bee.

"Hello, Ned. I'm glad to meet you. I'm Arnold Ant."

"Arnold left his anthill because he refused to work for the same pay as the other ants in his nest. So he decided to go it alone and look for cleaner pastures. He finally found what he was looking for right here," said Bobby Bee.

"Yeah, I worked twice as hard and put in longer hours than many of the other workers but the boss refused to pay me what I was worth. So I decided it was time to go," said Arnold Ant.

"Ned, I'm Gabby Grasshopper. I left my clan because I was tired of being teased and harassed by my peers for not chewing and spitting tobacco. I refused to put anything unhealthy into my body and I also refused to go out with the others to gorge on a human's harvest, just to bankrupt him and overtake his land. I have a conscience. I won't do it," he said.

"Yeah, and he never shuts up. He's constantly talking to himself or others," said Arnold Ant.

"I do not," said Gabby Grasshopper as he sat alone talking to himself.

"He does so. See. He can't keep quiet. He seems to have ants in his pants," said Bobby Bee.

"Hey. Watch what you're saying," said Arnold Ant.

"I'm sorry, Arnold – immediate ants excluded," said Bobby Bee.

"Thank you," said Arnold Ant.

"Ned, this guy is Willie Mud Wasp. He came to us just a few weeks ago," said Bobby Bee as Ned and Willie shook hands.

"Hello, Ned. I'm glad to meet you. I came here because I refused to live in the dirty mud. It's icky. I like living in hives like Bobby does," said Willie Mud Wasp.

"Ned, this handsome guy's name is Carl Caterpillar. I'll let him tell you the reason why he's with us and not at home," said Bobby Bee.

But Carl remained silent, not knowing what to say.

"Well Carl, are you going to speak or not?" asked Arnold Ant.

"You want to tell Ned your story or shall I?" asked Bobby Bee.

"I can speak for myself. Hello Ned. I'm glad to meet you. The reason I joined this group of rebel rousers was to find myself. I want to stay the way I am. I don't want to change," said Carl

The Hunt for Ned October

Caterpillar.

"Change? Change into what?" asked Ned.

"My family told me I had to go away and spin a cocoon and make a new life for myself. But I don't want to be a butterfly. I'm afraid of heights. I don't like to fly. I feel safe when all my feet are firmly planted on the ground. If you want to call me a rebel, so be it," said Carl Caterpillar.

"Here, here," cheered the bugs in unison.

"And this skinny guy is Pappy Praying Mantis," said Bobby Bee.

"Hi, Ned, I'm happy to meet you," he said.

"Why did you leave home?" asked Ned.

"It's a long story. But basically, I refused to pray their way. I believed in a different religion than my peers and they belittled and teased me for it. I would always question the elders' reasoning of life and they didn't like it. So I was kicked out of the group. That's why I left home and went on my own. But I'm glad I did. These guys are my new family now," said Pappy Praying Mantis.

"Bobby. You never told me why you're here. You're the first longhaired bee I've ever seen. In fact, you're the only bee I had ever seen until today," said Ned.

"Boy, aren't you lucky," said Bobby Bee.

"So tell me Bobby, why did **you** leave home?" asked Ned.

"I was tired of being teased by my friends. I didn't want to sting anyone. I'm a hippie bee and non-violent. I believe in peace and love, not hate and violence. I got tired of all the harassment so I left and ended up here with my new pals. You can join us if you want, Ned. We'd be glad to have you," said Bobby Bee.

"Bobby, I'd like to stay with you guys, but I have to find my way home. I know my friend Billy is worrying about me," said Ned.

"Who's Billy?" asked Arnold Ant.

"Billy's the boy who purchased me from the pet shop and placed me into the toilet," said Ned.

"How did you end up here, Ned?" asked Gabby Grasshopper.

"That's a long story. But basically, I was flushed down the toilet into the city sewers and I ended up here," said Ned.

"How are you going to get back home? Do you know the way?" asked Bobby Bee.

"I'm not sure. I was hoping you guys might be able to point me in the right direction. I know that my home is near the City Park. It's only a few blocks away from that area," said Ned.

"How do you know your home is near the City Park?" asked Gabby Grasshopper.

"When Billy was carrying me in my cardboard case to my new home, I could see through the little air holes in the sides of the box and I remember passing by the City Park," said Ned.

Just then, another one of the group's friends came flying into the campsite and Bobby Bee introduced Ned to the flying insect.

"Ned, this is Mickey Mosquito. He left home because he refused to bite humans. He was afraid of getting a disease. His peers thought he was a sissy and teased him like our peers teased the rest of us," said Bobby Bee.

"I'm glad to meet you, Mickey," said Ned.

"Boy, I almost didn't make it back here. I was nearly squished by human hands," said Mickey Mosquito.

"Mickey, we were just talking about Ned's dilemma. He was flushed down his owner's toilet and after many travels, finally ended up here. Now he wants to get back home and I think we can help him do that," said Bobby Bee.

"How?" asked Arnold Ant.

"Those of us that can fly will pan out and search the city for the park. Whoever finds it will return to the campsite and draw Ned a map to the area. In fact, we can even fly along with him and direct him to the park. How does that sound to you, Ned?" asked Bobby Bee.

"That sounds great. I can't tell you how much I appreciate your help," said Ned.

Just as the group was talking over a plan of attack, another flying insect zoomed overhead and into the campsite.

"It's about time you showed up, Nathan. I want to introduce you to a new friend of ours. This is Ned October. He's hoping we can help him find his way home. Ned, this shy guy is Nathan Gnat. He came to us after he had left home because he refused to feast on rabid and spoiled food," said Bobby Bee.

"That's right. I only eat healthy, organic vegetables," said Nathan Gnat.

"Ned, there's still a few of our group that aren't here. I'll introduce you to them at a later time. But I think it's time to put our plan into action," said Bobby Bee.

"What plan are you talking about?" asked Nathan Gnat.

"We are going to help Ned find the City Park. His owner's home is near that area. So if we can get him that far, he should be able to find his way home. Will you help, Nathan?" asked Bobby Bee.

"Sure. Whatever I can do," he said.

"Okay. Mickey, Willie, Nathan, and I will do our best to find the park, while the rest of you can stay here and keep Ned company. We'll return as soon as possible," said Bobby Bee and the four flying insects took off in four different directions.

CHAPTER 10

Four of Ned's new-found friends flew off to look for the City Park, while Billy, Tommy, and his neighborhood friends hung posters just a few blocks away. The two Russian spies were also close by, inspecting two turtles at the twentieth address that they had tracked down from the list Mr. Boyagian had given them. However, the Russian spies didn't see any of the flyers that Billy and his neighborhood friends had posted.

After checking the turtle at this address, the spies were now only three addresses away from Billy's residence. But they were only looking for one turtle at Billy's place. Nadene was a gift from Mr. Boyagian and wasn't on their list. So as far as the spies knew, Billy had just purchased one turtle and they weren't aware that he actually had two.

Billy, on the other hand, wasn't aware that the two Russian spies were interested in his turtles. In fact, he couldn't care less. He was only focused on finding Ned October. But in the back of his mind, Billy wondered if he would ever see his pet turtle again.

Billy was only blocks away from Ned, but didn't realize it. And just as Billy and his friends were leaving the City Park after hanging flyers for the past few hours, they were finally heading back home. They would hang more flyers the following morning.

As the boys exited the park, Bobby Bee had finally found what he had been seeking – the City Park. Bobby Bee quickly looked over the area, then in a wink of an eye, turned around and flew back to his campsite and told Ned the good news.

The other three flying insects had not returned yet. They were probably still out searching for the City Park. But Ned had little time to waste. He had been gone from home for too long as it was.

The Hunt for Ned October

He was ready for the long trip that would take him to the City Park and then hopefully to his final destination – Billy's house.

When Bobby Bee finally settled down and was able to catch his breath, he told Ned what he had found.

"Ned, I found the City Park. It's only a few blocks away. By air it only takes ten minutes to reach, but by land it may take days, or even weeks," said Bobby Bee.

"Can you draw me a map to help me find my way?" asked Ned.

"I'll do better than that. I'll fly above you and mark the way as we go along," said Bobby Bee.

"Aren't you forgetting something, Bobby?" asked Arnold Ant.

"Like what?" asked Bobby.

"Like Ned first has to maneuver through that horrendous minefield called the parking lot. It'll be a miracle if he can make it through that in one piece without being road kill," said Arnold Ant.

"Arnold does have a point, Ned. But, if you want to get home, you're gonna have to take that chance," said Bobby Bee.

"That's true. It's a wonder that I've made it this far still in one piece," said Ned.

"I wonder where the other guys are. Did any of them come back yet?" asked Bobby Bee.

"No. You're the first one to arrive. When they get tired or hungry, they'll be back," said Arnold Ant.

"If Ned does get through the parking lot in one piece, what will be his next obstacle that he will have to face?" asked Gabby Grasshopper.

"As far as I can tell, he will have to face four major obstacles. The first being the automaker's parking lot and the moving vehicles that whiz in and out at all hours of the day and night," said Bobby Bee.

"What are the other three?" asked Ned.

"Once you get past the parking lot, then you'll have to cross a major highway. But there is a part of the road that's being repaired where the traffic has to come to a complete stop until they are waved through the area by one of the workers. That's the second and deadliest obstacle after the parking lot," said Bobby Bee.

"Okay, so what are the other two? You said there were four obstacles that I would have to face. Tell me now, so I can make plans," said Ned.

"Well, the third obstacle is a river. You'll have to get around it by either crossing a bridge, or you could try swimming across the river, but the current's mighty swift. If you're not strong enough it could pull you downstream, and miles away from your target," said Bobby Bee.

"So I'll cross the bridge," said Ned.

"Except the bridge not only has cars and trucks crossing constantly, but it also has foot traffic," said Bobby Bee.

"What do you mean by foot traffic?" asked Ned.

"I mean the kids use it to cross to and from school. Not only is there a chance that you'll be demolished by motor vehicles, but you could also be trampled by scores of kids' feet," said Bobby Bee.

"There's no way Ned can bypass that bridge, is there?" asked Gabby Grasshopper.

"Yeah. I told you. He can swim across the river. But that will be just as rough as or rougher than crossing the bridge. Ned, you will have some brutal traveling to do whichever way you choose to go," said Bobby Bee.

"Well, that's three obstacles. If I get through those alive what's next?" asked Ned.

"You'll be lucky if you get through the parking lot alive," said Arnold Ant.

"Don't talk like that," said Gabby Grasshopper.

"Well, I'm only telling Ned the truth," said Arnold Ant.

"I know you don't mean any harm by what you're saying, Arnold, but like I said before, I came this far and I'm still in one piece. If I can make it through the jaws of monsters and surf on toxic chemicals and still be alive, then I feel I can take on any obstacles and be a better turtle for it. I have a plan for my future, and my friend Billy is part of it. Whatever it takes, I'm gonna push myself to the limit and never give up hope. If I believe hard enough, I know I can make it back home safe and sound no matter who gets in my way, or what I have to confront to do it. I'm going to move forward until either I reach my final destination or I end up in turtle heaven. At least I did my best. That's all anyone can ask of themselves," said Ned.

"Boy what a speech. I don't know what to say. I'm speechless," said Gabby Grasshopper.

"Gabby, you don't have to say anything. I want Bobby to tell me about the fourth and final obstacle that I have to pass. And that's just to get to the City Park. I still have nearly four blocks to go from there before I reach my final destination. And it's all busy streets. Not only will I have to confront moving vehicles, but I'll also have to maneuver through and around children's playing feet. I'm sorry to say, my long road home is just beginning," said Ned.

"I think I would have given up by now and made a new home for myself someplace else," said Gabby Grasshopper.

"Well, Gabby, that's the difference between me and you," said Ned.

"You could stay here with us. We'll be your friends," said Arnold Ant.

"Thanks, but I have my mind made up. I have to get back home to my friend, Billy. I know he's worrying about me as much as I'm worrying about him," said Ned.

Just then, Mickey Mosquito and Willie Mud Wasp came flying into the campsite and joined the crowd. A few minutes later Nathan Gnat fluttered into the campsite exhausted.

"What happened, Nathan? Why are you so tired?" asked Arnold Ant.

"I hit a strong headwind. The weather's changing. Winter is just around the corner," said Nathan Gnat.

"I think I hit that same headwind, too," said Mickey Mosquito.

As tired as the four flying insects were, they still joined in on the group's conversation.

"What are you guys talking about," asked Nathan Gnat.

"I was just telling Ned about the obstacles that he will have to get through to reach the City Park," said Bobby Bee.

"Oh, did you find it? I gave up looking for it. I absolutely had no luck at all. In fact, I'm lucky to be alive. First I was chased by a little bird and nearly splattered on a car windshield. Then, I hit that ghastly headwind. It's just not my day," said Nathan Gnat.

"It's not my day either. I looked high and low for the park but ended up in a gravel pit. The truck's exhaust fumes nearly killed me. That's why I turned around and came back here," said Willie Mud Wasp.

"Don't worry about it guys. I was lucky enough to find it. But now we have to figure out a way that Ned can get to the park without too much difficulty. But that doesn't seem likely. He's got many minefields to cross," said Bobby Bee.

"Minefields? We're not in a war. What are you talking about, Bobby?" asked Gabby Grasshopper.

"That's just an expression, Gabby. Ned will have some pretty tough territory to get through before he even reaches the park. Now we have to find the best route available," said Bobby Bee.

"Bobby, you were going to tell me about the last obstacle I would have to face before I reached the park. What is it?" asked Ned.

"I think the fourth and final hazard will be the worst. But depending on the time of day will make your task easier or more dangerous," said Bobby Bee.

"So, what is it?" asked Ned.

"It's a testing ground for college students to study lightning. These students put metal poles into the ground and then, using some type of discharge machine that makes static electricity, they are able to make lightning strike the poles," said Bobby Bee.

"So Ned will have to stay away from the metal poles. He shouldn't have any trouble with that obstacle," said Arnold Ant.

"That's not really true. The lightning throws out an electrical shock over nearly the whole area where the students are testing. Ned could be electrocuted if he's not careful," said Bobby Bee.

"You mean if he's not lucky," said Gabby Grasshopper.

"Ned will have to plan his route very carefully so he will go through the testing ground when the students aren't testing. That's all. If there aren't any lightning bolts then Ned won't have to worry about being electrocuted," said Bobby Bee.

"But don't those students test six and sometimes seven days a week?" asked Nathan Gnat.

"Yes, that's true. Ned will just have to wait for the right moment before he starts his journey through that minefield. That is the last obstacle that stands in his way to the City Park and freedom," said Bobby Bee.

"If I can make it to the park, then the rest of the way to my house should be a breeze. I only have a few streets and a cemetery to cross," said Ned.

"Well then, let's get started and draw up a plan. I'll also make a map for you that'll give you directions in case something happens to me while I'm in the air," said Bobby Bee.

"Are you going with him, Bobby?" asked Nathan Gnat.

"Yeah, I'm going to fly above him and show him the way. I'll be able to scout ahead and see if there are any hazards that Ned will have to face. That'll give us more time to bypass them," said Bobby Bee.

"I'll help too if you want. I could fly ahead of all of you and check out anything that catches my eye that I might think may be harmful to Ned's being. Then I could fly back and relay that information to you," said Nathan Gnat.

"If you want to tag along, be my guest. I'm sure Ned won't mind," said Bobby Bee.

"Not at all. I can use all the help I can get," said Ned.

"When are you going to start your journey, Ned?" asked Gabby Grasshopper.

"Bright and early tomorrow morning. If I don't get started soon, winter will be here before I know it. And I won't survive the snowy weather and cold temperatures," said Ned.

"Don't you hibernate in the winter?" asked Arnold Ant.

"I don't know. My mom and dad left me when I was a baby to fend for myself. That's when my little friend, Billy, saved me and gave me a home. I owe my life to him. That's why it's so important to me to get back home. I miss Billy very much," said Ned.

"You'll be home soon, Ned. I just know you will," said Bobby Bee.

"Don't worry, Ned. We'll help you get back home," said Nathan Gnat.

"Well, it's getting late and we all need our rest. We have to get up early to get Ned on his way. He should come to his first obstacle within an hour or two of starting out. He has to scramble through that big parking lot, only to confront the main highway. Ned definitely has his work cut out for him," said Bobby Bee.

The group of small critters snuggled around the campfire and fell asleep so they would be well rested for tomorrow's long journey to help Ned find his way home.

Chapter 11

Just as Ned and all his little friends were awakening to the new dawn, Billy was busy waking up his neighborhood friends so they could finish posting the flyers around the city.

While Ned and Billy were busy with their respective chores, the two Russian spies were busy tracking down the last few addresses, hoping to find the turtle that they had injected their precious microchip into. Most likely, they would reach Billy's address before nightfall. Billy was the twenty-third address on their list of twenty-five. So far, they had no luck finding their precious cargo.

In fact, Billy and his friends passed by the two Russian spies, crossing in front of the spies' car, while on their way into the city to hang flyers. The two spies still hadn't noticed or seen any of the flyers Billy and his friends had posted near the City Park and other nearby areas.

They were more focused on the addresses that needed to be tracked down. They believed that their precious cargo was in one of the turtles at one of the three addresses left on their list that Mr. Boyagian had given them.

Billy and his friends had posted flyers until they completely ran out of them. Just as they tacked up the last few flyers, a policeman walking the beat came up to them to see what they were doing.

"What are you kids up to?" asked the tall policeman as the kids stared at his big, shiny badge.

"Hello, officer. We are hanging flyers to find my friend's pet turtle," said Tommy.

"What's your name son?" asked the policeman.

The Hunt for Ned October

"My name is Tommy. This is Billy. He's the one who lost the turtle," said Tommy, pointing.

"Hello, Billy. My name is Officer Todd. Are Tommy and the other kids helping you hang up the flyers?" he asked.

"Yes. We just finished hanging the last one," said Billy.

"I see you are offering a reward for information leading to the return of your turtle. Is that right?" asked Officer Todd.

"Yes. Twenty-five dollars. I saved it myself. That was to be for my college education. But it's going for a good cause," said Billy.

"That's a very honorable thing to do, Billy. I wish you good luck in your endeavor. If I see a turtle that looks like the one on your flyers, I'll contact you as fast as I can. Now I must be going. I have to patrol the neighborhood," said Officer Todd, as he walked away.

"Thank you, Officer Todd," said Billy and the kids in unison.

It was nearly dinnertime before Billy and his friends returned home. Just as the kids began walking towards home, the two Russian spies had pulled up in front of Billy's residence in their Fish and Game truck.

After double checking the address, the two spies walked up and knocked on the front door. They were again dressed as Fish and Game inspectors looking for diseased turtles and using their miniature fluoroscope. They patiently waited until Marnie opened the door.

"Yes. May I help you?" asked Marnie.

"Yes, you can. We are from the Fish and Game department. I'm Inspector Tell and she's Inspector Moore. We have reason to believe that you purchased a small, green turtle from Mr. Boyagian's Pet Shop. Is that true?" he asked, as they showed her their phony identification.

"Yes. My son purchased a turtle there a few weeks ago. Why?" asked Marnie.

"We need to check your son's turtle for a very contagious disease," said Inspector Tell.

"What kind of contagious disease? Is it harmful to humans?" asked Marnie.

"It could be; especially to children. Although, we won't know that until we complete our diagnosis," said Inspector Tell.

"What if it doesn't have the disease? You won't hurt my son's turtle, will you?" asked Marnie.

"No. We have this miniature fluoroscope to check the turtle. It doesn't harm it at all," said Inspector Tell, as he held up the instrument.

"What if it does have the disease? What happens then?" asked Marnie.

"We will have to take the turtle with us and dispose of it," said Inspector Tell.

"Well I guess you have a job to do like the rest of us. Come in. I'll show you to my son's room," said Marnie, as she escorted the two Russian spies to Billy's bedroom.

Marnie stood behind the two phony inspectors while they checked Billy's pet turtle with their miniature fluoroscope. After two minutes they had completed their task and gave Marnie the all clear. The turtle wasn't the one the two spies were looking for. But they still had two addresses to check out so they were still confident that they would find their precious and important cargo.

Marnie escorted the phony Fish and Game inspectors to the front door and watched as they left in the truck that they came in. Marnie didn't show it in front of the two phony inspectors, but she was utterly relieved with the news that the turtle was free from disease. But she wasn't aware of the real reason those two people had visited her. If she had been, she would never have let them into her house in the first place.

Marnie also wasn't aware that Billy and his friends had finished posting the last of the flyers that Mr. Boyagian had made for him. At the same time, Tommy was trying to talk Billy into entering the sewers to look for Ned October.

While Billy was busy deciding whether he would go against his mother's wishes and look for Ned in one of the three large sewer drains, Ned was busy trying to cross the automaker's parking lot with the help of some of his new-found friends.

Bobby Bee, Nathan Gnat, Willie Mud Wasp, and Mickey Mosquito were flying overhead as Ned's air security team, watching for any harmful nuisance that might hinder his flight to freedom.

Grady Grasshopper, Carl Caterpillar, and Arnold Ant were Ned's ground security team. They were tagging along to keep Ned company and to communicate with the field commanders in the air.

Pappy Praying Mantis would stay behind to guard their campsite.

When Ned and his insect friends finally reached the cement parking lot, they were given the o.k. to continue their journey by his flying security team. Ned had already traveled for more than two hours from the toxic pond to the edge of the parking lot without any trouble from other predators.

The flying team saw a way for Ned and friends to bypass the dangerous parking lot and the monster vehicles that lived there, by walking around it and staying next to the fence line. But Ned would still have to cross a wide driveway that was used so vehicles could enter and exit the parking lot.

Going around instead of walking through, made for an extra long journey. But it was much safer this way. The only real threat was from a few scrawny birds looking for their next meal. But Ned's flying security team was able to shoo the hungry birds away and stop them from attacking Ned and his insect friends.

Once the birds were chased away, Ned was given the all clear from his flying security team to continue on his way. However, neither Ned nor the others were aware that the birds were now hiding within a large pine tree, patiently waiting for the right moment to strike down upon their prey. Ned and his insect friends, both the ground and air teams, were still in real danger. But that was an everyday occurrence for the insects.

Ned, however, never experienced any real danger, until he was sucked into the city's sewers and had to fend for himself. Nearly all his life, Ned was hand fed and treated like a king. He even had his own island to live on and his own lake to swim in. But lately, Ned had been living the life of a refugee – someone without a roof over his head or food in his belly. Ned believed that his luck would soon change for the better; especially with the help from his insect buddies. He couldn't have gotten this far without them and he knew it.

As Ned and his friends were given the all clear to continue their journey, they began inching along, crossing the wide driveway, which would bring them closer to the City Park. That was Ned's immediate destination before embarking on the second half of his trip on his journey home.

Nightfall would soon be upon Ned's group. As they inched their way across the driveway, the plant's whistle blew signaling to the workers that their workday had ended and that it was time for them to leave and head for their homes. Within minutes, thousands of vehicles were suddenly zooming past a frightened Ned October and his ground crew.

As the cars whizzed by, Ned quickly ducked for cover by hiding in his shell. The rest of his entourage stayed with Ned to protect him from harm. Luckily, Ned and his ground team stopped in the middle of the driveway so they were out of immediate danger, as long as none of the vehicles veered out of control and into their direction. Ned would have to wait for just the right moment and get the all clear from his security team in the air before venturing out again.

But Ned still refused to come out of his shell. He was very frightened and nobody could blame him. Ned was frozen with fear. When his air security team saw what was happening, they acted immediately and flew to Ned's aid without any fear for their own lives.

"Ned. Come on, snap out of it. Pull yourself together. If we all work together, we can get through this," said Bobby Bee, knocking on the back of Ned's shell to get his attention.

"I hear you, Bobby," said Ned.

Ned heard his friend's words and gathered enough strength to come out of hiding. Ned decided to give it his best shot and continue on his dangerous journey. With the help of his security teams, he knew when to move and when not to, so he wouldn't get smashed to bits by the tires of a motor vehicle leaving the automaker's parking lot.

By the time Ned and the others finally reached the other side of the automaker's driveway, the sun had nearly set. Ned and his friends began to relax, believing they were out of danger for the moment until they would have to cross the four-lane highway.

While Ned and his ground crew were taking a break, the air patrol went out to scout for the safest route possible and found a fairly safe area to cross at. They came across a road crew that was repairing the highway on both sides of the road not too far from Ned's rest stop.

Where the road was being repaired, traffic was slowed to nearly a dead stop. If Ned and the group timed it just right, they could weave their way through the congested traffic without too much trouble and very little danger.

But Ned and his friends decided to call it a day and make camp for the night. They were able to find shelter and warmth near some burning wood that had fallen out of a barrel. Some striking autoworkers had been using it as a stove to keep themselves warm in the nippy, fall air.

Ned and his team of insects slept near the glowing, hot embers of the fallen, burning wood until they were awakened by the automaker's loud whistle. By then the air team was already out scanning the nearby area. They were up when they felt the sun's rays on their little bodies.

Ned, however, was the last one to awaken from his deep slumber. He had walked more in one day than he had in his whole life. Every part of his body ached. Ned wasn't used to that much exercise. He wasn't in the best of shape. But, by the time he finished his long journey home, he would be in the best shape of his life.

Once the air team was certain of the route that Ned should take, Bobby Bee returned to camp to tell Ned and his ground crew.

"O.k., guys. Listen up. I think we've found the best way to go. We didn't talk about it last night. Everyone was too tired. But just up the road a piece is a perfect place to cross the highway. Ned, if you walk due east for about one hundred yards, you'll run right into the road crew that's repairing the road. When they stop the vehicles, that's when you can make your move and cross the highway, two lanes at a time," said Bobby Bee.

"That sounds good to me. Where's Nathan and Willie?" asked Ned.

"They're flying with Mickey, searching far ahead for anything that might hinder your journey home," said Bobby Bee.

"I really don't know how I can thank you enough for all the help you guys have given me. I'll remember you guys forever," said Ned.

"O.k., Ned. I have to get back with my team. So if you guys follow me, I'll direct you to the road crew," said Bobby Bee as he took off and flew high above looking down at Ned and the others, waiting for them to start the long journey towards the City Park.

As Ned crawled along slowly, Arnold Ant, and Gabby Grasshopper walked on either side of him, while Carl Caterpillar followed behind. But as Ned and his ground crew followed the trail set by Bobby Bee and his air team, they were unaware of the two scrawny birds perched high above in a pine tree, watching and waiting for the precise moment to make their move. The birds were desperate and hungry. They hadn't eaten in nearly two days and were anxious to dine on Ned and his insect friends.

Ned and his little entourage had only traveled a short distance when they were nearly trampled on by many pairs of striking autoworker's shuffling feet returning to fight for their rights. Luckily, Ned was able to dive for safety when he ducked into a small crevice and hid, while the workers ran past. But when Bobby Bee saw what was happening, he buzzed the men's heads and turned them away in another direction, which also helped Ned's ground crew scramble to safety without being injured.

When Ned and his ground crew were able to continue on their way, they thought they were out of danger. But the two scrawny birds had other ideas. Suddenly, the birds swooped down from their hidden perch and attacked Ned's little caravan. As Ned and his ground crew ran for cover, Gabby Grasshopper didn't move quite fast enough.

Using his strong, wiry legs, Gabby jumped high into the air, trying to evade capture. But he just didn't jump high or far enough.

"Help. Help," yelled Gabby Grasshopper, as one of the birds snatched him up between its beak in mid-air and carried him away.

Gabby's screams for help were quickly muffled, as he tried to wiggle free from his captor. But they were loud enough for Bobby Bee to hear and he came to Gabby's rescue by buzzing around the bird's head. Suddenly, Gabby's loud screams grew silent, as the bird whisked him away towards its domain. But due to Bobby Bee's actions Gabby escaped the bird's clutches and fell to the ground, returning to the group while the other bird was busy attacking Ned with its beak, pummeling his shell with ferocious nips and bites.

Ned had no safe place to hide so he retreated into his shell. By doing that, Ned hoped the bird would get frustrated and leave the area. But the bird refused to give up, wanting Ned for dinner.

When Bobby Bee saw Ned and his friends being attacked by another flying, feathery creature, he attacked this bird as it was attacking Ned. But the bird just ignored Bobby's antics and continued its attack on Ned. The bird attacked again and again, until it was able to grasp Ned between its beak and carry him into the air.

When Bobby Bee saw Ned being carried away, he gathered up all his strength and did something he had refused to do for his family. He put his little body into warp drive and made a beeline straight for the bird's behind.

As the bird carried Ned nearly five feet into the air, Bobby Bee jabbed his stinger deep into the bird's body. Bobby's poison began seeping through the bird's body, zapping the bird's strength immediately so it wasn't able to hold onto Ned. Within a few seconds after Bobby's stinger had hit its mark, Ned was dropped to the ground and was able to walk away uninjured because he landed on a mound of soft dirt.

However, Gabby Grasshopper wasn't so lucky. After escaping near death from the clutches of the bird, a small field mouse suddenly came out from the bushes and snatched Gabby between its jaws and disappeared into thin air. After a few screams for help, Gabby was never seen or heard from again.

When Ned and his entourage had reorganized and regrouped they were ready to start the march to freedom once again. But Bobby Bee was so concerned about Ned and his friends' welfare that he flew over to them to find out if they were all right.

"How's everyone doing, Ned?" asked Bobby Bee, as he settled among his circle of friends.

"We're alright. But Gabby didn't make it," said Ned.

"I thought I heard his screams. What happened to him?" asked Bobby Bee.

"He's gone. A furry field mouse took him away. I'm really gonna miss that guy," said Ned.

"How are you doing, Bobby?" asked Arnold Ant.

"I'm not feeling too well right now. I'm weak in the knees," said Bobby Bee.

"Bobby, I just want to thank you for saving my life again. I owe you my life," said Ned.

"Don't worry about it. I'm glad I could help. But I think I'd better return to my campsite to contemplate my future," said Bobby Bee as sweat poured from his body.

Ned knew when Bobby saved his life by stinging the predator

with his poisonous venom that Bobby would be going to bee heaven very shortly. Ned remembered Bobby telling him that the reason he left home was to escape the harassment from his peers when he refused to sting his enemies. But when it came down to it, he went against his own philosophy and saved Ned's life. Ned would never forget Bobby. He considered him a true friend.

"Thank you for everything, Bobby," said Ned.

Before Bobby Bee flew away to ponder his fate, he, Ned, and the others said a prayer and had a minute of silence to commemorate Gabby's passing.

"Good luck on your journey home, Ned. I wish I could be there to see Billy's face when he sees you," said Bobby Bee. He said no more and flew away out of sight.

A few minutes later, Ned and his ground crew continued on the trail that Bobby Bee had set for them. Nathan Gnat and Willie Mud Wasp were still out scouting the trail for Ned's journey and knew nothing about what had happened to Bobby and Gabby.

Ned suddenly stopped and stood silent for a few minutes wondering if he should continue on with his journey or turn back. But it wasn't a hard decision for him to make. He decided to go forward and not look back. If he turned back, his little friend's lives would have been lost for nothing.

Ned and his ground crew were on their own now, without the help of the air patrol. Nathan Gnat, Mickey Mosquito, and Willie Mud Wasp were still nowhere to be seen. Ned hoped they would return soon with information that would help in his journey home.

More than two hours had passed before Ned and his team reached the road crew repairing the four-lane highway. One human on each side of the highway was slowing the traffic almost to a standstill. This would be the perfect time for Ned and his friends to cross the road. But they would have to make double time if they wanted to make it across in one piece. If not, their tiny bodies would be splattered all over the road and left for road kill.

None of the members of the air team had returned to help Ned in his quest for freedom. Bobby Bee had been very helpful in that regard, coordinating the exact route for Ned's journey home. But now, Ned would have to count on his ground crew to get him through the rough times. Until the aircrew returned with some news, Ned wasn't certain if Nathan, Mickey, and Willie were even still alive. Ned was worried that they also might have met their demise while out scouting for him.

Ned put the bad thoughts out of his mind and concentrated on getting past this latest obstacle. The minute the road crew stopped traffic, Ned and his ground crew began their quest to cross the highway. But every time they reached a certain point, they were pushed back to where they started for fear of being demolished by traffic. They were able to maneuver only a few feet before the traffic would begin to move again. Luckily, Ned and his ground crew were able to turn and run before anything bad happened.

After four near misses, Ned and his friends were getting nowhere fast. They had to move back to the side of the highway and regroup to figure out their next move without getting smashed to pieces by the moving vehicles.

"What are we going to do, Ned? Every time we get halfway across the road, the traffic starts up again. This is beginning to be hazardous to our health," said Arnold Ant.

"Boy, I wish we had Bobby Bee scouting for us. He would have told us exactly when to go and when not to. Now we are like the blind leading the blind," said Carl Caterpillar.

"All we can do is what we've been doing. Hopefully, if nothing bad has happened to them, maybe Nathan, Mickey, and Willie will show up and get us through. They can see things in the air that we can't see on the ground," said Ned.

"Well. Let's give it another shot. I know we can cross this road. We just have to wait for the right time," said Arnold Ant.

When Ned and his ground crew agreed on a plan of action, they started out once again and began crossing the road when traffic had been stopped. But again, they were pushed back to the side of the road by overwhelming odds. They soon became disheartened, thinking that this was as far as Ned would get towards his final destination. But just as the group set out to try again, luck suddenly shined upon them. Nathan Gnat, Mickey Mosquito, and Willie Mud Wasp came flying to the rescue. When Ned and the boys saw them flying overhead, they were overjoyed.

"Where have you guys been? We were hoping you'd return," said Ned.

"Where's Bobby? Is he out scouting? We haven't seen him in quite a while. Do you guys know where he went off to?" asked

Willie Mud Wasp, as he, Mickey, and Nathan landed near Ned and his ground crew.

"Bobby Bee has left and returned to our original campsite to ponder his fate," said Arnold Ant.

"Why? What happened?" asked Nathan Gnat.

"While you guys were out scouting, we ran into a little trouble with some very hungry birds and a field mouse. Haven't you noticed that Gabby is no longer with us?" asked Ned.

"That's right. Where did he take off to?" asked Willie Mud Wasp.

"To a place where he didn't want to go," said Arnold Ant.

"What do you mean?" asked Nathan Gnat.

"He was taken by surprise by a cowardly field mouse when we were attacked by two, big, hungry birds," said Ned.

"How do you know he's not still alive?" asked Willie Mud Wasp.

"His fate was sealed when he was kidnapped by that little fat rodent. I'm afraid he's now in insect heaven," said Arnold Ant.

"That's too bad. I really liked old Gabby. But what happened to Bobby Bee? Did he run into the same trouble?" asked Willie Mud Wasp.

"Kind of: When he saw us getting attacked by the birds, he came to our rescue and did something that he had promised himself he would never do," said Ned.

"And what was that?" asked Nathan Gnat.

"He used his stinger and attacked the bird that had me in its grasp. When Bobby stung the bird, he saved my life because the bird dropped me and flew off. But I'm afraid Bobby's fate was sealed also when he went against his own philosophy to save my life. He is a true friend and I'll never forget him. I pray that he'll recuperate but I know that he won't," said Ned.

"I'm sorry to hear that. Bobby and Gabby were very good friends of mine," said Nathan Gnat.

"Unfortunately, this is part of life. We have to take the good with the bad. But I'll tell you one thing. They'll always be in my thoughts and prayers," said Willie Mud Wasp.

"Here, here," said the group in unison.

"Let's not dwell on the past. Let's look to the future. I saw the trouble that you and your ground crew were having trying to cross the highway. You weren't making very good progress. Ned, I think

I've found a way for you to bypass your latest obstacle," said Mickey Mosquito.

"How's that?" asked Ned.

"Just about twenty yards up the road is a small drain pipe that runs completely underneath the highway and it's just large enough for you and your ground crew to get through without much trouble," said Willie Mud Wasp.

"Lead the way, Willie. That's what we've been waiting for. Now that Bobby Bee is gone, you, Mickey, and Nathan will have to stay close by and show us the way. Flying above, you have an advantage. You can see things that we can't," said Ned.

"Don't worry. I'll stick to you like glue. Nathan and Mickey can fly ahead and scout the area and look for any other trouble that you might run into. I'll stay near you and point the way from overhead," said Willie Mud Wasp.

"Let's get going then. Time's a wasting. I want to make up for lost time," said Ned, as he and his ground crew began their trek to the drainpipe.

After a few short hours, Ned and his fine team of bodyguards reached the underground drainpipe. They began their long walk through the dark cavern, while Willie Mud Wasp and Mickey Mosquito flew overhead, waiting for their friends to reach the other side of the highway. It was very slow traveling but after a few more hours Ned and his team finally came to the end of the tunnel.

By the time Ned and his ground team had overcome the second obstacle of their long journey, the sky had blackened and darkness had fallen upon them. They decided to make camp and wait for daylight before starting out again. Their third obstacle was nearly one hundred yards away and would take them practically a whole day just to reach. Then Ned would have to decide whether to cross the bridge or swim across the river.

Ned and his ground crew huddled around their warm campfire and left all their worries behind. Within a few minutes, Nathan Gnat, Mickey Mosquito, and Willie Mud Wasp had joined them. But the group remained silent. They were either too tired or saddened by the day's misfortunes. One by one, they quickly fell asleep.

Ned and his team were up before daylight, ready to begin the day's hard journey towards the next obstacle in their path. Willie Mud Wasp, Mickey Mosquito, and Nathan Gnat had already flown off to scout ahead, while Ned and his ground crew were busy making leaps and bounds to their next goal. It was in the late afternoon when they finally reached the bridge.

After a brief discussion with the others, Ned decided to try the bridge. He and his ground crew would use the sidewalk as their fastest route to get across the bridge. Everything went as planned. There was very little traffic on the road and even less on the sidewalk. So Ned and his team thought they would be in the clear. But before they traveled less than halfway across, things started to go bad.

Again, Ned and his team were confronted by shuffling feet. This time, it was the feet of happy children running home from school. To get out the way of the trampling feet, Ned was forced to jump into the river far, far below.

But as Ned jumped off the bridge and began falling Arnold Ant and Carl Caterpillar hung onto him for dear life. They were gonna stick with Ned through thick and thin. They grabbed onto his shell while they pummeled to the river below.

As Ned and his ground team were falling, Willie Mud Wasp saw what had happened and flew to their rescue. Willie flew underneath and pushed up against Ned's shell, trying to slow his fall or at least soften it. But Ned was falling too fast and Willie's heartfelt actions were too little, too late.

Suddenly, Willie's life was in danger. He had to act fast to get out of the way of Ned's falling body or he would have become a statistic like Gabby Grasshopper and Bobby Bee.

Then suddenly: **splash**. When they hit the raging water, Carl and Arnold were thrown a few feet away but Willie came out of it with only wet wings. Ned was in bad shape though. He wasn't unconscious like the other times he had fallen, but he had his breath knocked out of him and couldn't breathe for a short while.

As Willie Mud Wasp flew overhead, Carl and Arnold quickly swam back to Ned and held onto his shell as they floated in the water. But as they were floating on the water, waiting for Ned's strength and energy to return, they were suddenly confronted by a group of sharks. Actually, the circling predators were Largemouth bass, looking for lunch. When Carl and Arnold saw danger lurking, they jumped onto Ned's back and began using Ned as a life raft.

As Ned bobbed up and down with the waves, Carl and Arnold sat on Ned's back, holding onto the edge of his shell, riding the waves as though they were riding a bucking bronco.

Ned surfed the raging water's erratic waves as though he had been doing it all his life. But as he came within sight of shore, the wind suddenly picked up and nearly blew Carl and Arnold back into the water. Luckily, they were holding onto Ned's shell tight enough to weather the course. But the wind blew Ned farther and farther downstream, until the bridge was completely out of sight.

Willie Mud Wasp tried to intervene and use his stinger as a rope for Ned to hang on to, but Ned bobbed up and down too much in the rough surf and couldn't make contact with Willie's stinger. Willie had to give up and watch helplessly as Ned and his friends drifted farther and farther off course.

Just as suddenly as the wind raged, it died down enough so Ned could finally make it to land. But he was miles from the route Bobby Bee had laid out for them. By the time Ned, Arnold, and Carl had finally reached land, the sun had already set. Even though they had lost precious time, they decided to camp for the evening and dry out.

Nathan Gnat and Mickey Mosquito, however, had no way of knowing where their friends were. They were following the route that had been set down before they had left their campsite on the automaker's property.

Willie Mud Wasp began worrying about Nathan and Mickey and flew off to see if he could find his friends. Although it was nighttime, there was a full moon that lit up the starry sky.

As Willie was flying east, Nathan and Mickey were flying west. Within twenty minutes, they had flown within a few feet of each other.

"There you are. I've been looking for you guys," said Willie Mud Wasp.

"Where did you go, Willie? When I couldn't find you, I thought something bad happened to you and that maybe you had gone to insect heaven. I guess I was wrong," said Nathan Gnat.

"You sure are. Follow me and I'll escort you guys to our campsite," said Willie Wasp.

Ned's air team flew back to the campsite wanting some much-needed sleep. Nathan and Mickey had scouted the route all the way to the park and then returned, flying non-stop into strong head winds.

When the group thought they had found refuge and a safe haven near the raging river's edge, they would soon learn differently. The light from the group's campfire and the glow from the moonlit night brought out predators from every direction.

Awakening from a deep slumber, Ned and his insect friends quickly became aware of the area's animal population. Their campfire was being overrun by many different types of furry creatures – a mother raccoon and her three baby raccoons, a smelly skunk, a red fox, a large, sly, alley cat, a homeless dog, two field mice, an old owl and a large bat, which Ned had seen before in the sewer.

To Ned and his group it was as if they were defending the Alamo against the warring foreign soldiers. But there were just too many of them. The first predator that the group was confronted with was the mother raccoon and her three babies. They were out foraging for food. As they entered camp, Carl and Arnold ran and hid in the tall grass at the edge of the river, while Willie, Mickey, and Nathan took to the skies.

But just as the three flying insects thought they were free of their enemies, they quickly found themselves dodging an annoying bat. As Willie, Mickey, and Nathan flew in circles around trees and tried other deceptive maneuvers to get out of the path of their antagonist, Ned stood his ground and stayed by the campfire, retreating into his shell while waiting to be pounced upon by the raccoons. But they never came into camp. They sniffed the area but were soon chased away by a large, roving dog.

When the dog sniffed Ned's shell and clawed at him with his paw, he quickly became disillusioned and ran off for better game. As the raccoons and dog ran in opposite directions to each other and away from Ned's campsite, Arnold Ant and Carl Caterpillar returned to Ned's side.

When the bat became bored with chasing flying insects, he decided instead to go after the two field mice that had been wandering near Ned's campsite. So Willie Mud Wasp and Nathan Gnat were able to return to camp but Mickey Mosquito wasn't as lucky. When Mickey took flight, he put his body into warp drive to escape the intruders and flew so fast that he wasn't able to control his flight. He ran smack dab into a tree, splattering himself beyond recognition. When Willie and Nathan found him, they knew he was beyond help. Mickey's soul had already gone to insect heaven.

They were about to tell their story to Ned and the others when two small, furry creatures once again interrupted them. In fact, Ned and his friends would have been dinner for them, but instead, the small, furry creatures were being chased off.

Ned and his air and ground crew were just starting to relax around the fire when the two mice ran through the camp, trying to escape the wrath of the hungry bat, as Nathan and Willie had a few minutes earlier. As the mice ran through camp, Ned's security teams ran or flew in all directions, trying to get as much distance as they could between them and their hungry predators.

After a long, torturous race, one of the two mice lost the game. The bat caught his dinner and quickly flew back to its dwelling. As the other mouse ran for cover, Ned and his friends, once again, returned to their warm, glowing campsite but weren't sure if they'd ever get any sleep on this particular night.

After saying a prayer and having a minute of silence for Mickey, Ned and his friends tried getting some well-deserved rest, hoping the excitement had passed for the night. Unfortunately that wasn't the case. The large dog that had chased away the raccoons earlier that evening suddenly returned and ran past Ned's campsite, as it chased after a big, old alley cat.

Minutes after that the mouse that had run for cover and had escaped the bat's wrath was now being chased by an old owl that had been watching from his perch high in a nearby tree; this time the innocent mouse's luck ran out when the owl pounced on it and took him away.

Ned and his friends couldn't believe the chaos that had erupted around them and wondered if there would be any other outbreaks of violence. Finally, they realized that if they stayed in that particular area they would never get any sleep. So they put out the campfire and began walking back up river, closer to their original route. They decided to make a new campsite in a safer area and hopefully out of the prying eyes of their ferocious enemies.

But as Ned and his ground team silently walked along the

river's edge, a smelly skunk ran past being chased by a red fox which was also being chased by the same dog that had earlier been chasing an old alley cat.

When the skunk sprayed its smelly perfume at the red fox, the wind blew the foul smell directly over Ned and his ground crew. Luckily, Willie Mud Wasp and Nathan Gnat had already left the group to search for a more peaceful place to set up camp.

After nearly two long hours, the flying team directed them to a large, sandy area and Ned and his little friends found a good spot to make camp. Ned and his insect friends were so tired that none of them wanted to start a fire. They were afraid that other predators would be drawn to it, so they decided to make do without it. Instead, they were warmed by the bright glow of the starry heavens.

Luckily, Ned and his little friends weren't bothered by anyone the rest of the night. They slept soundly until the early morning when they were awakened by chirping birds on a cloudy, dreary, drizzly day.

Willie Mud Wasp and Nathan Gnat left the group immediately and flew off to find the route that they had lost sight of the day before. Ned and his ground crew quickly broke up camp and began their travels towards their final destination – the City Park.

During the two-hour walk the night before from one campsite to another, Ned and his ground crew were able to make up almost all of the distance they had lost the day before. But they still had one more obstacle to face before they would reach their goal and that was the electrical minefield that college students used to study lightning bolts. They would have their work cut out for them.

The cold, chafing wind and the drizzling rain made this part of Ned's journey very dangerous. December was fast approaching and the weather was changing for the worse.

Ned's time to find his friend, Billy, was running out. He didn't want to get caught in the cold, freezing temperatures during the winter months. That was the time many of his peers went into hibernation, but Ned was abandoned at birth and never told the facts of life. He didn't know the first thing about hibernation. So Ned only had a week or possibly even days to find his way home.

By that afternoon the winds and rain picked up. Ned and his

ground crew were very near the electrical minefield when Willie Mud Wasp returned to the group to tell them what to expect.

"Ned. We got problems," said Willie Mud Wasp.

"What's up?" asked Ned October.

"Along with the weather making its own lightning bolts, the college students are still testing and trying to make their own. You're gonna have to be very careful not to step into the path of those lightning bolts," said Willie Mud Wasp.

Ned had been hoping that the students weren't testing and that he could walk through the electrical field without any problems. They would still have the threat of predators to contend with but wouldn't have to worry about getting blown apart by a lightning bolt. At least they had hoped luck would be on their side. But that wasn't to be.

The minute Ned and his ground team stepped into the electrical minefield, they were confronted by one lightning bolt after another. They were shooting down from the rainy and darkened, cloudy skies and struck just a few feet away from them. The electrical blast was strong enough to stop Ned and the others in their tracks.

All twelve feet of Carl Caterpillar were being shocked and burned so much by the electrical charge produced from the lightning bolts that he jumped on Ned's back to lighten the burning sensation to his feet. Arnold Ant did the same as the electrical shock was too strong for his little feet, too. Now the electrical shock would go through Ned's body instead of theirs.

But one lightning bolt's shock wave was so strong that Ned's body began to smolder and smoke as steam began to rise from his little, green shell. It got so bad that Ned's ground crew yelled out for Willie Mud Wasp's help.

When Willie heard the screams, he turned his afterburners on and flew back to Ned in record time. He saw Ned, Carl, and Arnold in dire need of help. They were huddled together, steam was rising from their bodies, and they were pleading for him to get them to a safer area.

"What's wrong?" asked Willie Mud Wasp as he flew above them.

"What does it look like? We're being roasted alive. Will you help us get out of here?" asked Ned.

"I guess I'll have to, Ned. If I don't, we'll soon be serving roasted turtle, toasted ant, and crunchy caterpillar," said Willie Mud Wasp as he hovered just above his burning friends.

"What do you want us to do?" asked Ned.

"Ned, I want you to grab hold of my stinger and hold on tight. Let's see if I can't lift you out of this electrical minefield," said Willie Mud Wasp as he tried with all his might to lift Ned, with Arnold and Carl holding onto Ned's back.

But the three of them were just too heavy for Willie to lift them out of harm's way. He tried again and again but couldn't keep them in the air long enough to get them to safer ground. He could lift them a couple of feet off the ground but after just a few short minutes, his strength would give out and he had to drop them back to earth.

Just as Willie dropped Ned and his passengers for a third time, a fierce lightning bolt came out from the darkened, cloudy, rainy skies and struck so close that the shock wave knocked Willie out of the air and onto the ground. He hit the ground so hard that it took the wind out his sails. But the electrical charge produced from the lightning bolt was strong enough to shock him right back to his feet.

All of a sudden, three college students came running out of their testing shed where they measured the electrical fields produced from the lightning bolts, nearly trampling Ned and the others. But luckily, Willie had heard the students' shuffling feet and reacted swiftly.

"Ned, grab on," said Willie Mud Wasp as he quickly took to the air. Ned held onto his stinger for dear life, and Carl and Arnold held onto Ned.

With one giant burst of great strength and energy, Willie was able to lift Ned, Carl, and Arnold to safety; which was on the other side of the electrical testing grounds. Now Ned and his group had only fifty yards to go before they reached the City Park's boundaries. Once there, Ned hoped to find his bearings that would point him in the right direction home. Then he could walk the last leg of his long journey.

Once Ned and his ground crew were out of danger, they rested just long enough to energize their batteries for their long trek to the City Park. While they rested, Willie Mud Wasp flew off to search for Nathan Gnat and to seek out any other danger that might be lurking in the shadows.

Ned was just hours away from the City Park. He was unaware that his owner, Billy Smith, was already there with Tommy and the other neighborhood boys. Tommy had talked Billy into searching one of the three sewer drains that emptied into the City Park's lovely pond. Billy was hesitant at first, not wanting to go against his mother's wishes, but decided to forgo his mother's orders and search the sewers for his little friend, Ned October.

Chapter 12

By late afternoon, Ned had finally reached the City Park thanks to the help from his family of insect friends that he had met during his long road home. Tears were flowing from all of them.

Nathan Gnat and Willie Mud Wasp returned to the edge of the park to say goodbye to their close and dear friend, Ned October. By their joyous reaction, they were happy to see that Ned had made his journey to his planned destination all in one piece. Even though they had lost Bobby Bee, Gabby Grasshopper, and Mickey Mosquito, they were still overcome with joy. They were very happy for Ned. Now they hoped his road home would be a safe one.

As Ned and his insect friends gathered around in a small circle, Ned gave thanks to the ones that helped him in his quest for freedom.

"I just want to thank you guys for helping me. I couldn't have done it without you. I know I owe all of you, including Bobby Bee, Mickey Mosquito, and Gabby Grasshopper my life. I'll never forget you as long as I live," cried Ned October.

"It's been our pleasure, Ned. We were glad to be part of your entourage during this long, exciting journey. We'll never forget you, either," said Willie Mud Wasp.

"Here, here," said the others in unison.

"I'm going to get all misty if I say anymore," cried Ned, teary eyed.

"Good luck on the rest of your journey, Ned. Do you have a plan for the last leg of your trip home?" asked Arnold Ant.

"I haven't thought that far ahead, yet. I still have to find my bearings and then head in the right direction. My home is only a few blocks away from here. Just over there is the pet shop that I was purchased from," said Ned, as he pointed straight ahead.

"We would like to tag along and help you find your way to the Promised Land but winter is near and we have to return to our campsite. We have to make preparations for the coming months or we'll be left out in the freezing cold," said Willie Mud Wasp.

"Don't worry about it. I'm just thankful that you were able to help me this far," said Ned. He shook his little friends' hands and then hugged each one of them goodbye.

Before Ned could say another word, Arnold had jumped onto Willie's back and Carl onto Nathan's back, and then they flew off into the wild, blue yonder.

While Ned was waving goodbye to his insect friends, the two Russian spies drove past the City Park in their phony Fish and Game truck, unaware that the turtle that held their precious microchip was just a few feet away in the grassy knoll.

The phony Fish and Game inspectors had just checked the last few turtles on their address list and were disappointed and confused that they didn't find their precious cargo. But as they drove past the park, they noticed the flyers that had been posted on many of the park's trees showing a reward leading to the return of a pet turtle called Ned October.

The truck suddenly veered off the road and stopped. The female spy jumped out and snatched one of the posted flyers from its place and quickly jumped back into the truck showing her partner the flyer, which also contained the name and address of the turtle's owner. When the two spies saw that the address was one that was on their list and one that they had already checked out, they decided to return there and question the homeowner about the lost turtle.

The two spies sat along the side of the road debating if the lost turtle was the one that they had already checked with their miniature fluoroscope. But when they looked over the flyer again they saw the date that the turtle had disappeared, and it corresponded with their timetable.

"Are you sure that this is the turtle we are looking for?" asked the female spy, Nadia Romanelski, alias Inspector Moore.

"I don't know. But I promise you, one way or another we are going to find out. We will know once we question this woman,

Marnie Smith," said Boris Kolavski, alias Inspector Tell.

The two Russian spies pulled their truck back onto the road and sped off towards the address on the flyer. They needed to find out if the missing turtle was the one that held their precious microchip. They were sure it would be him. It had to be. That was the last known turtle to be sold at Mr. Boyagian's Pet Shop.

Neither Ned nor Billy was aware of the two spies' intentions. Ned was busy making plans for the last leg of his journey and Billy was busy with the other boys, searching one of the park's sewer drains.

With flashlights blaring, Billy, Tommy, and the others were running and playing in the shallow, polluted sewer waters. They came to a junction of multiple sewer drains and were trying to decide which one to take. Suddenly a bat flew overhead and scared the daylights out of them.

While the boys were protecting their hair and heads from the furry, flying vampires that were attacking from above, they were also confronted by another fear. This one was that same three-foot alligator that Ned had confronted days earlier. As the boys screamed in terror, they turned and ran as fast as they could into another big sewer drain not knowing exactly where it would lead them, but hoping it would lead them away from the ugly creature with the massive jaws and very sharp teeth.

Even though Billy and his friends searched high and low in the sewers for Ned October they had no luck finding him. They believed he was still lost in the city's web of underground sewer pipes, but that wasn't the case. Ned was nearer than they thought. He was only fifty yards away on the other side of the park.

While Ned was looking for a place to rest, Billy, Tommy, and the other boys were exiting one of the City Park's sewer drains, opposite of Ned's direction. Neither Ned nor Billy noticed one another or knew that they had been just fifty yards away from each other.

But Billy and the boys decided to come back to the City Park another day to search the third and last sewer drain. There wasn't enough time to do it now. Darkness was falling so the boys had to make double time to get home before dinner so their parents wouldn't become angry with them for being late. The boys made it home in record time but Billy noticed visitors when he entered his home. It was the Fish and Game inspectors and they were asking his mother some questions about his lost turtle.

"So Mrs. Smith is it true that your son purchased this turtle only two weeks ago?" asked the phony Inspector Tell showing her the flyer.

"Yes. That's true," she said as Billy looked on and listened to what was being said.

"Why didn't you tell us this when we were here a few days ago?" asked the phony Inspector Moore.

"You never asked me about another turtle. You only asked if my son had purchased a turtle from Mr. Boyagian's Pet Shop during the last two weeks. I told you he did and that was the truth," said Marnie.

"But Billy purchased two turtles. Didn't he?" asked the phony Inspector Tell.

"No, he didn't. He purchased one and when that one got lost, he was given another one from Mr. Boyagian. So my son only purchased one turtle during that time, so what I told you was the truth," said Billy's mother, Marnie.

"I'm sorry we didn't make ourselves clear when we first questioned you. Now that we have it cleared up do you know where this other turtle is? We need to check him like we have all the others that were sold from Mr. Boyagian's Pet Shop," said the phony Inspector Tell.

"Billy, have you found Ned October yet?" asked his mother, as Billy moved closer to the adults.

"No. I'm still looking. But I won't give up until Ned's back, safe and sound," he said.

"So young man, you have no idea where this Ned October is? How did you lose him? And where did you lose him?" asked the phony Inspector Tell.

"That's a long story," said Billy.

"We have time. So tell us son, what happened to your pet turtle?" asked Inspector Tell.

"He was flushed down the toilet into the city sewers. I looked for him in a couple of the sewer drains but I haven't had any luck yet. But I will," said Billy.

"Billy, I told you not to go into those sewers. You disobeyed me. Why?" asked his mother.

"I'm sorry, Mom. I know I shouldn't have gone against your orders, but Tommy talked me into it."

"Billy, do you know what sewer he was flushed into?" asked Inspector Tell.

"No, not really. But three of them come out at the City Park and so far we've searched two of them. We were going to search the other one tomorrow, but now I guess I won't be able to," he said.

"Mrs. Smith, you would be doing us a big favor if you allow Billy to continue his hunt for Ned October. He would be doing mankind a favor. Especially, if he were to find him," said Inspector Tell.

"Well, if you think that's best. But young man, you and your friends be very careful when you search those sewer drains. They are very dangerous. I don't really want you to go into them, but if these inspectors need your help, I guess it will be all right. But I want you home before dinnertime. Is that understood, Billy?" asked his mother.

"Yes, Mom. I understand. I'll be extra careful and I promise I'll be home before dinner," said Billy, as he walked happily into his bedroom.

"Well then, Mrs. Smith. I guess we have taken up enough of your time, so we'll be going. But we'll be keeping in touch over the next few days. I just hope your son is lucky enough to find his pet turtle. I know it's important to him but it's more important to us. Ned October is the last and final turtle from this batch that needs to be checked for that contagious disease," said Inspector Tell. Then he and his female partner walked out of the house and drove away to figure out their next step in locating their precious cargo.

"Boris, what is our next move?" asked his female partner, Nadia.

"Nadia. We have to follow Billy, without his knowledge of course, in the hopes that he will lead us to the Promised Land. If he finds the turtle, we'll be able to check it and salvage our microchip and our lives."

While the two Russian spies were making their plans for redemption, Ned was busy making friends with the park's friendly inhabitants. The first animal he met was a friendly rabbit that was busy making its winter's nest.

"Hello. I'm Ned October. How are you doing?" he said.

"Hi. I'm Rebecca. I'm trying to get my home completed before the snows come. I should be finished with it in another few hours," said Rebecca Rabbit as she continued adding soft material to her nest.

"I'm going to be around for the next day or so. I'm trying to find my way home," said Ned.

"Why don't you make a home here? We have a lovely pond," said Rebecca Rabbit.

"I see that. But I don't want to make my home in a pond when I have a warm house waiting for me," said Ned.

"What's wrong with our pond? There's plenty of room to make a nice winter's den here," said Rebecca Rabbit.

"I'm sure there is. But I have a home already," said Ned.

"Where is that?" asked Rebecca Rabbit.

"It's a few blocks from here. When I find a certain landmark, I'll know which way I'll have to go to get to my owner's house," said Ned.

"Which landmark are you talking about? Maybe I've seen it," said Rebecca Rabbit.

"It's a small water fountain right near a row of mail boxes lined up on one corner of the main street that leads directly to my home. Once I find it, I'll know the way," said Ned.

"I've never seen the mail boxes or the fountain. I'll ask around. Maybe one of my other neighbors has seen the landmark you're talking about," said Rebecca Rabbit.

"I'd really appreciate that," remarked Ned.

"When I see Dimmer Duck, I'll ask him. He flies all around this area. I'm sure he's seen the fountain you're talking about," said Rebecca Rabbit.

"Thank you. I better let you get back to work. I think I'll go check out the pond," said Ned, then began walking in that direction.

"When I get through with my work, I'll take you around to some of my neighbors and you can ask them about the landmark you're seeking," said Rebecca Rabbit.

Ned continued towards the pond as night grew near. The rain had stopped but the wind was rather chilly. But Ned's energy was turned towards a glowing, barbecue pit. When he reached the area there were still many hot coals on the ground that had not been rained upon. Ned made a bed near the hot coals by quickly stacking a few fallen leaves together.

Ned felt relieved that he had gotten as far as he had and still was alive and in one piece. But he knew he still had a long way to go before he reached his final destination. However, at this particular moment, he only wanted to relax and get some much-needed sleep. So Ned closed his eyes and fell fast asleep only to be awakened by Rebecca Rabbit.

"Hey, Ned, are you awake?" asked Rebecca Rabbit.

"I am now. How did you find me?" asked Ned.

"I saw your campfire and when I got a closer look I noticed you resting in your bed. So I thought I would stop by and see if you wanted to visit a few of my neighbors," said Rebecca Rabbit.

"Rebecca, I'm really tired tonight. Would you be angry if I asked for a rain check?" asked Ned.

"No. I won't be mad. I understand," said Rebecca Rabbit.

"We could visit your neighbors in the morning," said Ned.

"That's fine with me. I just thought I'd see how you were doing but I guess I'll let you get back to sleep," said Rebecca Rabbit as she walked away.

Ned quickly fell fast asleep and was awakened the next morning by Rebecca Rabbit.

"Ned. Are you awake yet?" she asked

"Yep. I'm up," said Ned, as he opened his eyes, jumping out of his leaf bed.

Rebecca wasn't alone. She had come to visit with one of her neighbors, a mallard duck.

"Ned, I'd like you to meet one of my neighbors. This is Dimmer," said Rebecca.

"I'm glad to meet you, Dimmer," said Ned.

"Are you Ned October? Are you the turtle that's lost?" asked Dimmer Duck.

"Yeah, how did you know that? Did Rebecca tell you?" asked Ned.

"No. She didn't have to. I saw your face and name on flyers that are posted all over town," said Dimmer Duck.

"You've got to be kidding. Are you telling me people are looking for me?" asked Ned.

"That's right. You're a celebrity," said Dimmer Duck.

"I'm on my way home right now. But I need to find a fountain and row of mailboxes near a corner street. Rebecca told me you might know where they are. Do you?" asked Ned.

"No. Not off hand. But when I'm flying, I'll keep my eyes open," said Dimmer Duck.

"Thanks, Dimmer. I need all the help I can get," said Ned.

"That's why I brought Dimmer here. I thought he could help you," said Rebecca.

"If you don't mind me asking, how did you get a name like Dimmer?" asked Ned.

"My friends think I'm a little dimmer up here than they are," he said, pointing to his head. "So they started calling me Dimmer and it just stuck," he added.

"Ned, I thought we could take a walk around the park and meet my other neighbors. What do you think?" asked Rebecca.

"I would, but I need to jump in the pond and take a bath. Then I have to start searching for that landmark. If I don't find that soon, I'm gonna end up being stuck here for the winter and I'll never survive living outside in the freezing cold," said Ned.

"Well maybe you can meet my neighbors later this afternoon. I'll stop by later and see if you're busy. That is, if you don't mind?" said Rebecca Rabbit.

"No. I don't mind. But I can't make any promises," said Ned, as Dimmer and Rebecca walked away.

Ned walked to the edge of the pond and jumped in. The cold pond water perked him right up. In the middle of the pond was a small island that caught Ned's curiosity. So he swam over to see what was there. He thought he would be alone on the island but he would soon find out that there were others living there.

As soon as Ned hit the island's shoreline, a crowd of angry geese met him. They didn't want him anywhere near their island. They threatened to have him for a snack if he didn't leave at once. So Ned obliged the quacking geese and slipped back into the pond. He retreated as fast as he could to a safe haven of Lilly pads just a few yards from shore. But there he was met by a number of huge, croaking bullfrogs yelling at him for invading their territory.

"Right now we're busy eating flies and insects but our diet could change to turtle if you don't get out of here and fast," said the elder bullfrog. He leapt from one Lilly pad to another to get a closer look at their intruder.

"I'm sorry. I didn't mean to invade your territory. I thought I was living in a free country. I guess I was wrong," said Ned, as he swam away for greener pastures.

But as Ned swam towards shore, he was unaware that a large fish that was his natural enemy was stalking him. When Ned finally noticed the giant fish swimming after him, he swam as fast as he could. Ned thought his life was over when the fish leapt out of the water straight for him with its massive jaws open and ready to snatch him up into his mouth and swallow him whole.

But luckily for Ned, a hawk flying high above the trees saw the whole episode unfold.

So when the hawk saw the fish jump out of the water after Ned, he dove down and snatched it up in his claws and took it away. Thanks to the intervention of the hawk, Ned was able to swim safely to shore and out of harm's way. Ned was so tired from this latest ordeal that he slowly dragged himself onto shore and collapsed from lack of breath.

But as Ned rested to gather enough strength and energy to move, he was overrun by a group of young boys running towards one of the park's three large sewer drains that emptied into the park's pond. If Ned hadn't reacted quickly and jumped back into the water, he would have been squished by a number of trampling feet.

Ned dove deep into the water and by the time he came up for air the group of boys was far away, on the other side of the park, just entering the sewer drain. That's when Ned thought he had heard one of the boy's yell, "Billy." Ned wasn't sure if he had heard right and wondered if the boy had yelled his owner's name. Ned would have to wait until the boys returned to see if he had heard right.

Ned finally exited the pond and began walking to his makeshift campsite to relax and think about his future plans to find his owner's home. As he walked to his campsite, he could see many of the park's inhabitants making their winter homes so they could get through the cold months without freezing to death. Ned waved to them as he passed by on his way to his campsite but they just ignored him and continued working on their winter homes.

When Ned reached his campsite he was happy to see that many of the coals that had fallen out of the barbecue pit were still glowing and still very hot, which helped Ned dry out. He lay back down on his bed of leaves to think and ponder his fate. Two minutes later however, his thoughts were interrupted when Rebecca Rabbit stopped by to talk with him.

"Hey, Ned, are you busy?" she asked.

"Not really. I'm just catching my breath," he said.

"I know. I saw everything that happened to you out in the pond. I was watching you from my place," said Rebecca Rabbit.

"What did you see?" asked Ned.

"I saw Gandara chewing you out for coming on her property," said Rebecca Rabbit.

"Who's Gandara?" asked Ned.

"She's the goose you had the run-in with on the island," said Rebecca Rabbit.

"Oh yeah. She's not very friendly," said Ned.

"Don't worry. She hates everybody. She even hates herself. But don't worry. She's flying south soon," said Rebecca Rabbit.

"She needs anger management classes," said Ned.

"So does Bully," said Rebecca Rabbit.

"Who's Bully?" asked Ned.

"He's the Bullfrog that yelled at you for climbing onto his Lilly pad," said Rebecca Rabbit.

"He wasn't very friendly either. Nor was that fish that attacked me," said Ned.

"I saw that too. I think the one that attacked you was Peter Pike. We've had lots of trouble from him over the years. But he won't attack anyone anymore. Harry saw to that," said Rebecca Rabbit.

"Is Harry the Hawk that saved me?" asked Ned.

"That's right. You're lucky he was in the right place at the right time," said Rebecca Rabbit.

"I sure am. When I see him I'll have to thank him," said Ned.

"If you want we can stop by his place. That's why I stopped by. I thought I would introduce you to some of my friendly neighbors. Do you feel like visiting or are you too tired?" asked Rebecca Rabbit.

"No, I'm not too tired. I'll go with you, but only for a little while. At least it will take my mind off my troubles," said Ned.

"What troubles?" asked Rebecca Rabbit.

"I shouldn't have said troubles. That was the wrong word. It's just that I have to work out my plans for the last leg of my journey home before it gets too cold. Winter is just around the corner," said Ned.

"Don't I know that. My winter home is nearly complete. If you want I'll help you make your winter home?" asked Rebecca Rabbit.

"No thanks. I appreciate the help but I have a home just a few blocks from here. I just have to find out in what direction," said Ned

Rebecca and Ned began walking towards a neighbor's place.

"We'll stop by my best friends place first. She's my cousin. Her name is Rita Rabbit. She's going to be a mother in a few more days," said Rebecca Rabbit.

"That's nice," said Ned as they stopped in front of a large bush.

"Rita. It's Rebecca. I want you to meet a friend of mine," she said, as her cousin stuck her head out of her den hidden by a large bush.

"Hello, Rebecca. How are you?" asked Rita.

"Rita, I'd like you to meet a friend, Ned October. He's a celebrity. His face is the one on the flyer that everyone is looking for. He's trying to make his way home before winter sets in," said Rebecca Rabbit.

"I'm glad to meet you, Ned," said Rita Rabbit.

"I'm glad to meet you, Rita," said Ned.

But as Rita and Rebecca began a conversation, Ned's interest was interrupted by a group of boy's loud noises.

Ned heard the boys screaming as they were exiting the park's drain sewer and looked to see if his friend, Billy was among them. He turned and walked away from Rebecca and her cousin to see if he could identify any of the boys. But Ned was too far away to see any of the boys' faces clearly. So he ran towards them as fast as his little legs would carry him. He was only thirty feet away when he heard one of the boy's call out the name of Billy. But Ned still couldn't identify any of the boys, including the one they called Billy.

Ned had nearly caught up to the group of boys until they suddenly bolted from the park's playground. But Ned had been close enough to see that one of the boys was his friend and owner,

Billy Smith. However, before Ned could yell out his name, the boys ran out of the park and stopped at the street corner.

Ned continued running after Billy but was no match for their speed and thought his chase was all for nothing. But then the boys were stopped by a traffic light, which gave Ned another chance to reach them. Ned quickly turned his after burners on and ran faster than he ever had before. But to no avail.

Just as Ned reached the sidewalk, he saw a Fish and Game truck roar past and then heard loud screams, a car horn, screeching brakes and a loud thump. Ned couldn't see Billy and his friends and figured they had already run into the street and had disappeared into the large crowd that had gathered around a fallen boy. It was Billy.

Ned was too far away to see who had been injured and when he tried to get closer to the scene of the accident, he was chased away and nearly stepped on by hoards of moving feet. To get out of the way of being trampled to death, Ned was pushed out into the street, near a pothole that had just been filled with hot, tarry asphalt. As he stood ten yards from the accident, he was suddenly being pelted by hot blobs of tar that were being spit out of the tar machine as it boiled over.

As Ned ran to get away from being tarred to death, he was nearly hit by a car as it rumbled past, but when he car's rear tire hit the pothole that had just been filled with the hot tarry asphalt, a big glob of it stuck to its sidewall.

The car's rear tire passed by so close to Ned that it sucked him up into the tarry substance. As the car rumbled down the street, Ned spun round and round much faster than he had swirling down the toilet. He tried his very best and fought with all his might to escape the deadly, dizzying ride but had no luck until a few miles later when the car's rear tire hit another empty pot hole. Ned was thrown fifty feet into some bushes on a grassy knoll overlooking a small pond but on a smaller scale.

When Ned was able to move his injured, weary body, he somehow found a way to get down from the bushes. But Ned was frightened by his new surroundings and hid under a large, broken branch until he was sure it was safe to leave. Ned scouted the area for predators and when he was satisfied that he was out of danger, he pushed himself towards the pond to wash his bruises and battered body.

Limping along the grassy grounds, Ned saw many of the small Park's inhabitants were busy making their winter homes, like his in the City Park. When Ned finally reached the pond, a rather rough raccoon confronted him.

"What are you doing in my territory? Did I say you could be here?" asked the raccoon in a deep, booming voice.

When Ned looked up to see who was dogging him, he noticed many of the park's inhabitants were listening to their conversation.

"I'm sorry. What did you say? asked Ned, while he washed his face and feet in the pond's cold water.

"I told you to get off my property, unless you want to suffer the consequences," said the angry raccoon.

"I'm sorry. Let me introduce myself. I'm Ned October. Maybe you heard of me?" he asked."

"So what if I have? I'm Ronny and I'm the law around here. What I say goes. Understood?" he asked.

"Ronny, I'm glad to meet you. I don't want any trouble. If you've heard of me, then you know that I'm lost and I'm trying to find my way home," said Ned.

"How long do you plan on being around here, Ned?" asked Ronny Raccoon.

"I hope to be out of here as soon as possible, except I don't know where I'm at. I was at the City Park just a few minutes ago and now I'm lost again," said Ned.

"You're quite a ways from the City Park. In fact, you're about two miles North of it. How did you get here? asked Ronny Raccoon.

"Let's just say I hopped a ride on a car. But it took me in the opposite direction of where I wanted to go," said Ned.

"Well just keep your nose clean while you're here. We don't allow any troublemakers around here. You make trouble, you're outta here. And I mean for good. Get me?"asked Ronny Raccoon as he thumped his chest with his paw.

"I understand. As soon as I'm able, I'll get out of your hair. But right now I have to rest and heal my aching body," said Ned.

"Just remember, I'm going to keep my eyes on you," said Ronny Raccoon, as he walked away.

The Hunt for Ned October

Ned found a spot under a Pine tree, made a bed out of discarded pine needles and rested his road weary body. He had hoped to leave the area within a few days and begin his long journey home but things didn't go as expected. His fragile body didn't heal as fast as Ned had wanted and a few days turned into more than a week. During this time, the weather had changed drastically and turned for the worse. It became freezing cold at night.

When Ned was kidnapped by that tarry, roving, spinning wheel and thrown into the bushes, he was injured worse than he realized. From that day forward he was very depressed over not being able to find his home. He had no insects to help him and the park's inhabitants weren't very friendly, so he stayed to himself.

One day, in the early part of December, Ned went for a swim in a small pond. He was on the far end and had just begun his swim to shore when a blizzard suddenly fell upon the area. Within minutes the pond's water began freezing over. Ned had gotten within a few feet from shore when he suddenly became frozen solid into the ice.

Luckily for Ned, the same group of boys that he had seen and had chased at the City Park were now running around and playing on the ice within feet of his frozen, little, green body. Every boy but one. And that was his friend and owner, Billy Smith. He wasn't anywhere to be found. But Ned was frozen in the ice and wasn't aware of anything.

The two Russian spies, however, were very aware of the boys. They had been following them in their truck, hoping that they would find the lost turtle that held their precious microchip. The two spies parked on the side of the road and watched as the boys played on the ice

As one of the boys skated in Ned's direction, he noticed something dark in the ice. When he went over to investigate he was surprised to see a little green turtle.

"Hey, guys. Look at this," said Ned's finder, as the other boys gathered around the dark object stuck in the ice.

"Tommy, what is that?" asked one of the boys in the group.

"Jimmy, I think it's a turtle. In fact, I think it might be Billy's pet turtle." exclaimed Tommy, as he began scraping the ice with a stick, trying to free the little, green turtle.

"You mean, Ned October?" asked Jimmy.

"That's exactly who I mean," said Tommy as they brought Ned to the surface.

"Will Billy be able to recognize him? I mean, ever since he got hit by that truck near the City Park he hasn't been the same," said Jimmy.

"You wouldn't feel the same either if you had lost your pet turtle and then ended up in the hospital from being run down by two foreigners. And remember, Ned helped pull Billy out of his coma, too," said Tommy.

"Tommy, do you really think it's Ned October?" asked Jimmy as the boys looked at the turtle in Tommy's gloved hands.

"I don't know. Why don't we take it to Billy at the hospital? He would be able to tell or not if it's Ned," said Tommy.

But Ned was still frozen and hadn't thawed out yet.

"Is he still alive, Tommy? asked Jimmy.

"I think so. But I can't really tell," said Tommy.

"Will he thaw out?" asked Jimmy.

"I'm not really sure. But I think so," said Tommy.

"What do you want to do? Take it home? asked Jimmy.

"The hospital is just around the corner. Let's take the turtle to Billy and ask him if it's Ned October. Maybe by the time we get there Ned will have thawed out," said Tommy, placing Ned in his shirt pocket. He and the other boys then ran to the hospital just a few blocks as the two Russian spies followed slowly behind in their truck.

Tommy and the boys reached the hospital in record time. They entered through the revolving doors and rode the elevator to the seventh floor where Billy was staying.

However, the boys were unaware that two Russian spies close by lurking near Billy's room had followed them from the park.

Tommy checked the turtle to see if it had regained its senses but it hadn't. So he placed it back in his shirt pocket as he and the boys walked to Billy's room. Just before they entered the room, Tommy checked the turtle once again for a sign of life but it still seemed frozen so he held it in his hands as he and the boys entered Billy's room.

"Hey, Billy, we've got a surprise for you," said Tommy as he and the other boys walked into the hospital room, unaware that the spies were listening from outside the door.

"Boys, don't' be so loud," snapped the nurse.

Billy's right leg and left arm were still in traction after he was nearly run over by a truck right near the City Park. He was the one injured the day Ned saw him. Billy had been very depressed since the accident because he still had not found his little, pet turtle, Ned October.

"Hello, boys," said Billy's mother, Marnie.

"Hello, Mrs. Smith," said the boys in unison.

"What brings you to the hospital?" asked Billy's mother.

"We've got a surprise for Billy. This should put a smile on his face," said Tommy as he held out his hands and showed him the turtle he had found.

Billy remained silent but looked intently at the little, green turtle. It had a spot or two of tar on the top of its shell, looked weather beaten and wasn't moving. But Tommy still placed it upon Billy's chest.

Within a few seconds, Billy reached for it with his good hand and picked it up, then held it close to his bandaged face. The second he picked it up to look at its bottom shell, the turtle began moving its legs, as though it was swimming. Practically, at the same time, Billy saw that the turtle was the one he had lost and the turtle saw that the boy was his long lost friend, Billy Smith.

"Ned, it's YOU, It's really YOU!" cried Billy as he held Ned close to his face.

Ned licked Billy's face and was happy once again, as was his owner and best friend.

Boy, they would have some stories to tell each other.

But things suddenly turned for the worse. When the two Russian spies heard Billy scream out Ned's name, they immediately stormed into the room in their phony Fish and Game outfits.

"We'll take that turtle, if you don't mind," demanded Inspector Tell, walking up to Billy's bed, holding out his outstretched hand.

"No! You can't have my turtle. I just got him back," cried Billy, holding Ned away from grabbing hands.

"You must give us that turtle. We have to check it for a disease. If it doesn't have it, then you can have it back. Just let us check it," said Inspector Tell.

"Billy. Give him the turtle. He has a job to do. He checked Nadene for the disease, let him check Ned," demanded Billy's mother.

"All right, Mom. If you say so," said Billy, as he handed the turtle over to Inspector Tell.

The second Inspector Tell had Ned in his grasp and checked it with his miniature fluoroscope to see if the turtle was the one that held their precious microchip inside its tiny body, a smile crossed his lips. The news was very upsetting to Billy.

"I'm sorry, Billy. But your turtle has the disease and we'll have to take it and destroy it. I wish I could have given you better news," said Inspector Tell. He nodded to his female partner and they quickly departed the room with Ned October in tow.

"Please don't take Ned. Please!" cried Billy, as he watched the two phony Fish and Game inspectors leave the room.

But just as the two inspectors walked through the doorway, they were intercepted by three United States Federal Officers and taken into custody as spies.

After nearly two weeks, once the micro chip had been retrieved and given to the proper authorities, the spies were deported back to Russia, and Ned was returned to Billy and they both lived happily ever after.

The moral to this story is that if you work hard, believe in yourself and in what you're doing and never give up hope, your dreams will come true.